Shadow Women

Homeless Women's Survival Stories

Marjorie Bard, Ph.D.

Sheed & Ward

Sheed & Ward™ is a service of National Catholic Reporter Publishing
Company, Inc.

Library of Congress Catalog Card Number: 90-60897

ISBN: 1-55612-358-2

Published by: Sheed & Ward
                  115 E. Armour Blvd. P.O. Box 419492
                  Kansas City, MO 64141

To order, call: (800) 333-7373

2/07

Contents

Introduction

They spend nights hidden in cars, cemetery crypts, and buildings under construction—or openly in such twenty-four hour havens as Atlantic City hotel-casinos, transportation terminals, and coffee shops. They spend days in malls, libraries, and hospital complexes. They eat their way through grocery stores, use coupons for free or inexpensive food, and "dine-and-skip" in busy restaurants. They are clean, dressed and coiffed neatly, and seem serene. They look and act like "normal" shoppers, gamblers, dawdlers, and visitors, but *"they"* are solo homeless women—mainly over forty years of age and surprisingly well educated—who blend into polite society. These "shadow women" may roam from place to place or establish a relatively permanent daily routine within any radius that suits waking and sleeping needs. I found (and still find) them in all urban and suburban areas: uptown, downtown, crosstown, beach; touristtown, tracktown, port town, and retreats.

I know them and their ways because I was one of them. I escaped a nomad life when I was accepted at UCLA for graduate study, and financed by grants obtained an M.A. and a Ph.D. (My doctoral dissertation focuses on the topics of domestic abuse and homelessness correlated to organizational and community involvement.) During my academic days I also worked at a shelter for battered women, acted as a victim advocate in the Los Angeles City Attorney's Office, and founded an organization to provide direct services to pre-homeless and homeless women. Currently I assist other organizational representatives in efforts to design, fund, and implement programs and projects for abused and homeless women. Consequently, this book is a fifteen-year field journal of women's

v

personal experience narratives concerning why and how they became and remain homeless. The stories reflect community and system responses and needs.

While public and private sector personnel and researchers pursue quantitative and qualitative information-gathering regarding the urban homeless in America (with conflicting data and inferences), there is a dearth of knowledge related to the lone homeless woman who is neither unmistakeably and/or dysfunctionally mentally ill nor highly visible as a streetscene, mission, or shelter member. There is also little information regarding those "urban" homeless who dwell on the fringes of cities—not strictly within the boundaries of what we label city or town, but not properly classified as "rural." They straddle what academics and professionals carefully try to divide: urban, suburban-urban, suburban, and rural. A large number of homeless individuals travel from one community to another, staying for varying amounts of time in what may be within a city's limits only to move on to find refuge in suburbia-bordering-on-country—and then return to what cannot be denied as an "urban" area.

The qualitative material presented in this book about a population of homeless women who have been heretofore unperceived and therefore unexposed points to a significant rise in any quantitative data about homeless people. There are obviously large numbers of people who escape the censustaker, professional, and academic. In addition, this material provides new inferences concerning who is *and may become* homeless; there are millions of housewives, widows, and employed women who do not even suspect that they are "at risk."

The women whose stories appear here continuously engage in ingenious methods for finding safe shelter, seeking daily sustenance, and practicing some form of financial gain. They define "innovation," and we respect a self-reliant, survivalist attitude. Each woman indicates that she communicates problems and visions to herself and selected others to maintain personal dignity and identity *and* an acceptable public image. We all understand that need;

we do the same. But psychologically, spiritually, socially, and economically these women are on the brink; some will continue to balance precariously between self-sufficiency and the dreaded mission or street syndrome, some will slip into a downward spiral never to regain current standards, and others appear to be creeping back up the ladder to a possible reintegration into mainstream life. Strategy seems to be the root metaphor for survival. Disguise (or perhaps "camouflage"), composure, and guarded conversation combine as a public mask. Sturdy-and-stylized department store bags, large purses, and clothing with voluminous pockets substitute for the dead giveaway: the shopping basket filled with belongings (although recently I note the use of very fashionable fabric-covered carts). Many homeless women have keys to private lockers, and some have post office boxes, bank accounts, and safety deposit boxes.

Almost all of such homeless women have been responsible for ownership or rental of houses or apartments in the past (as opposed to having been dependent on a parent). The majority are not only high school graduates but have some college background (and an astounding number have bachelor's degrees, master's degrees, and Ph.D.s); and while over 75% have been housewives, only a few have not had any experience in some formal workingplace environment. Most of the women refer to becoming "overnight indigents," but a large number drift into a static or nomadic lifestyle after sporadic attempts to live with relatives or friends. Some are victims of the act(s) of one or more persons, while others have experienced dual victimization: by individual(s) and "the system." It is interesting to note that while almost all are articulate about economic, political, social, and religious systems, the information which they have about Social Security, Disability, and other government benefits is too often incorrect. Whether they were provided with that misinformation (and thus became victims of "the system") or deduced it themselves is usually unknown; the important fact is that many *could* be receiving a monthly stipend which could alter their circumstances. With all of their background differences, they end up with one thing in common: they have become borderline members of society who are always in our midst but remain either unrevealed or incognito to all but the occasional confidant or other homeless women who see a reflection of themselves.

I am of two minds about this book. I am divulging the secrets of survival for innumerable women who dwell in semi-privacy and desired anonymity. I fear that I am betraying not the confidences regarding the situations and behaviors which have brought them to their current status, but the manner in which they are staying alive and relatively sane. We do not expect people to be *dwelling* in the spaces used in transience for the pursuit of business or pleasure— especially in the most exclusive sections of town. But we are becoming desensitized to those who do not exactly "fit in" in any locale, for dress codes are flexible, hair styles are acceptably idiosyncratic, and behavior is coded to loosely defined scenarios. Consequently, it is particularly easy to overlook the homeless woman who can harmonize with the environment by playing a part: strolling a mall with assumed purchases; sitting quietly, reading in a library; walking market aisles nibbling on finger foods and sipping a soda; waiting patiently for transportation; utilizing free cosmetics while browsing in a store; testing recliner chairs next to a television department; spending many hours in a cool church on a hot summer day; idling away the day in a park or bowling alley; or enjoying casino life. I respect the obscurity which they nurture; they have designed and developed a way to live with as much dignity as possible. Yet I find myself shining a light into the shadows —highlighting the women, the ways in which they exist, their social and psychic states, belief systems, economic enterprises, and the politics which affect them.

I do this for four reasons. First, if *I* do not reveal what I knew as a homeless woman and have learned from others, who will? It is not the kind of information that anyone can offer. Even when on special assignment, newspaper and magazine reporters have to depend on highly visible populations—or a few informants who have been discovered and have nothing to lose by being interviewed. Academics can try to gather ethnographic data, but cannot give up years to "become a homeless person." Further, academics and reporters know they can always return to the safety of a home; theirs is a clockwork world. I had the distinct "advantage" of being part of this specific population—which led to specific insights, e.g., knowing how to identify and approach individuals who wish to remain anonymous. Even so, I had to be extremely flexible. I usually told "my story" to elicit stories—and listened with (uninterrupted) interest to life experiences shared by others. Making good use of the shorthand I was forced to learn as a teenager, I wrote on a pad inside of a large purse; scribbled on napkins, placemats, bags, and even a skirt; and "doodled" on a large calendar I carried as part of my own personal baggage. When I realized that I wanted to hear the women's voices and the whole of our conversations at some point in the future, I bought two small tape recorders and a lot of tapes and batteries. When I could, I put the machines in plain sight; when I could not, I left a bag or purse open so that the recorder was partially hidden. At first, of course, I did not know to what use I might put my growing database, but I was positive that the personal experiences of homeless women were to be valued. In the 1970s (while I was living on the East Coast) I collected nearly 400 stories. During immediately following years (on the West Coast while in graduate school and working in both private and public sectors) I documented another 1500. That sounds like a lot. (Approximately) 2000 stories *in fifteen years* is *not* a large amount when one considers that in every major city there is an alarming increase in the number of crisis calls to missions and shelters, city and district attorney's offices, and associated public and private agencies for a wide variety of free and/or inexpensive services: immediate shelter as well as longer-term affordable housing, jobs and job training, emergency and maintenance health care, legal assistance, and so on. (In Los Angeles *County* alone, 2000 stories *every year* is an underestimate.) Smaller cities and suburban areas also note a disturbing rise in voluntary and involuntary homeless people. Most women who do receive assistance find that it is temporary and inadequate and eventually they fall through some crack in a system during any stage between having a home and living on the streets. We must note that women who contact public and private agencies reflect only a *fraction* of those who experience poverty, victimization, and/or homelessness; there are large numbers who never contact any person or any agency. I have met women who fit into all of those categories, and I have been able to assist only a relatively small number. I continue to identify the about-to-be and currently homeless, searching for the themes and motifs which explain such a rapid rise in (solo) homeless females.

Second, just as so many Holocaust victims swear they have only lived to tell their stories to the uninformed, for personal and historical reasons, I discovered that my informants feel much the same way. They want others to know what has happened to them, but almost all have experienced rejection (or worse) and are now wary of strangers as well as "the system." What occurs, then, is the conscious process of *solitary* storytelling (which is what we all do as a natural response after an encounter which is so noteworthy that it is silently reconstructed as a prelude to telling others). This may become one's primary means of communication: to self, who cares. In victims' accountings, "I" is the protagonist, having been denied not only compensation (payment for past damage), but indemnification: consideration of self as worthy of a present and insurance for a future. Inherent in expressiveness which involves one's "self"— alone or in relationships—is concern with that which can be called personhood, upon which Albert Jonsen elaborates (in *Humanities Network*, Vol. 9:1 [1987]):

> We talk about the maintenance of life; we rarely talk about the maintenance of personhood. It is of very little interest to me to be alive as an organism. In such a state, I have no interests literally. It is enormously interesting for me to be a person, with my history, with my place in life, doing the things I enjoy doing, loving those I love, causing the problems I like to cause. I live my life. It is the perpetuation of my personhood that interests me.

The first-person ("I") narrative also projects truth to an otherwise strange or unbelievable experience. It has been utilized universally throughout time as a tool to persuade, educate, entertain, anger, sadden, and admonish. Throughout this book one can hear women using the personal experience story to accomplish all such means of influence.

The opportunity to tell one's story may never arise, and some stories are secrets which are assumed will never be shared (because of shame, guilt, or the desire to protect someone). Stories initiated are often affected by selected editing, being cut-off in progress, and misinterpretation leading to story disintegration. Consequently many life stories *remain* silent and internalized: "one's own," idiosyncratic, and private storytelling sessions. While such commonplace self-narrating is in part cathartic and even therapeutic, one result of what appears to be the constant solitary characterization of traumatic events is that which we may see and judge as "mentally ill" behavior: the public display of chattering and gesturing to an unseen audience. We notice it especially among the highly visible homeless. The fine line between idionarrating (which is soundless, in the way of reminiscence and reverie) and audible discourse apparently disappears and the individual may not be aware of the emergent sounds at all. The story needs to be told in any manner at all, for we are biologically coded, culturally prescribed, and socially trained to tell stories: *homo sapiens* is *homo narrans*. All too often I learned that I was the first person to hear the story(ies) a woman wanted to tell and not been so abled, and there was always an expression of gratitude: a hand reaching to grasp mine, tears, a verbal "Thank you for paying attention to me," a tangible gift of some personally meaningful kind, or an outpouring of other stories which were symbolic of our shared intimacy and trust. People not only need to tell about their personal experiences, they need and appreciate the interest of a listener other than "self." Therefore, even one confidant may be enough to perpetuate personhood and sanity in an otherwise friendless world.

Third, while the personal narratives of homeless women are autobiographical, they are also oral historical—compelling commentaries on societal life, whether performed in manner crude or refined, clever or pedestrian, prudent or brash. During the course of narrating about past events and her present means of survival, each woman is revealing that which defines the status of many urban/suburban females in the 1970s and 1980s (and undoubtedly the 1990s). It is improbable that these stories, which are representative of personal, social, religious, ethnic, cultural, economic, legal, judicial, ethical, and political standards and practices, will be included in history books. Oral histories, then, are very important primary source material for "written" history.

Fourth, and perhaps the most important reason of all, is that these homeless women not only describe (in their storytellings) the manner in which they have become marginal members of society and are surviving despite disturbing inabilities and injustices, they posit *solutions* to problems which exist in the public and private sectors which may be unrecognized, underestimated, ignored, misunderstood, and/or mismanaged. The ragged edge is often the cutting edge: these women are able to articulate insights and information regarding specific causes of homelessness; the correlations between psychological abuse, unresolved anger, and illnesses; spiritual disintegration; strategies for self-sufficiency, and suggestions for grassroots activism concerning changes in social and public policy. They talk about social responsibility and justice. The fact that they are living in virtual exclusion from public policy-making is testimony to the belief by mainstream men and women that these particular victims cannot define relevant issues.

While researchers who focus on homelessness mean well, they too often presume, label, categorize, standardize, conclude, propose, and predict by utilizing their own presuppositions, assumptions, and conceptualizations: their values and attitudes are not necessarily those of the victims. Victims who have become *organized* (e.g., Mothers Against Drunk Drivers) feel that they understand victimization, needs, and activist strategies better than those who only view from a distance and return to their clock-determined worlds. What there *is* in the way of victim input in public policy is achieved only because of organizational clout. But there are no organizations comprised of homeless women to raise a united voice or to send representatives to coalition meetings, and it should be apparent why this is so: communication—networking—between such victims is limited by personal, economic, and spatial factors and therefore mainly (but not exclusively) to the selected sharing of information as to where to find free food, safe sleeping places, and unlocked bathrooms with soap. However, those urban/suburban homeless women who are successfully surviving in anonymity do have a sense of what can be accomplished. Their innovative suggestions for preventive homelessness, self-reliance, confrontation, and remedy would add greatly to present programs and policy. It will be noted that there is a strong voice among our storytellers that the so-called "women's movement" has let them down—actually done nothing at all about the growing homeless female populations. There is an implicit if not explicit call to the mainstream *churchwoman* to begin where the National Organization for Women and National Coalition Against Domestic Violence members have left off; a national *churchwomen's movement* to alleviate and perhaps eradicate this increasingly pervasive societal problem is proposed. To emphasize the importance of female Christian leadership, many homeless women have paraphrased biblical passages and lectured me on the duty of "feeding the hungry" (Luke 1:46-56) and "associating and sharing with those in need" (Romans 12). Catholic women have recited the Magnificat and stressed the significance of Mary as a role model who represents the marginal woman who may be victimized and homeless as well as a visionary to create social change. Women of all creeds appear to believe that women are natural organizers and problem-solvers, and that those who are the religious are the hope of the homeless.

As a result of the above four reasons, I reveal that which may worsen the lives of women who are surviving as opposed to having died, and in many cases, bridging the gap between mere life and meaningful existence. That gap signifies the maintenance and perpetuation of personhood. By piercing the shadows which protect dignity, I am removing a particular type of support system. But I can no longer remain silent—or rather, I can no longer keep *their* voices silent. There are just too many homeless women. Because I engaged in lengthy, multiple storytelling sessions with many of the women, it would be impossible to include everything exchanged. However, I have not interfered with communicants' language except to delete the ever-present (and certainly not restricted to homeless women's discourse) "ers," "and ums," and "ahs" that detract from easy reading. (The scholar in me was intrigued by the idea of attempting to design a way for readers to "hear" individualistic accents and other idiosyncratic features, but I could not maintain consistency since not all interviews were taped. And such reading might be rather difficult as well.)

Interestingly, what is often judged as a lapse or departure from a topic during the telling of a story is almost always a purposeful tool: an explanation, description, excuse, apology, clarification, correction, or addition, and therefore I have included everything that was said in specific time frames unless noted otherwise (elipses denote material deleted). It has been in those very "digressions"—which other researchers may have deemed unimportant or off the subject—that I have discovered some of the most salient and intriguing insights. The reader will learn of such techniques as food acquisition, van decor, and health care as an integrated part of stories which are meant to be commentary on some other topic—such as organizational politics. Reconstructions of religious or frightening experiences which explain particular mental states and/or public rejection seem to be blended without hesitation into stories of, for instance, legal problems or economic strategy. Consequently, personal demons may only emerge within other stories—those which characterize the causes and lifestyles of homelessness. I have not separated the stories within the stories—the surrealistic from the realistic—for each woman proffers her own life history as a gestalt: the emotional, physical, social, religious, and political self. This presented a challenge as to how to chapterize the stories. I settled on first revealing where and how these solo homeless women are currently living, and then I focus in turn on their innovative economic ventures, the "politics" which they define as instrumental to their status, the disturbing problems they describe concerning our public sector agencies and systems, the traditional and religious experiences which are expressed as affecting personhood, and finally, the breakdown of each preceding chapter into a discussion of *solutions*. The last chapter leans heavily on a very special call to service to the churchwomen of America. By organizing, resourcing, and webworking on local and national levels, it is believed that churchwomen can serve those who are the neediest so that they in turn may serve others; a servant-leader model exacts the best from us: it exhalts the "perpetuation of personhood."

An excellent example of a successful servant-leader model (*my* appraisal of their concept) is Habitat for Humanity, a privately-funded, volunteer-based organization founded in Americus, Georgia, in 1976, by Millard Fuller. This now international movement challenges committed people to "solve" poverty, inadequate housing, and homelessness by joining with society's least advantaged to build (from scratch) extremely-affordable housing; in other words, the religiously-motivated assist needy individuals who are willing to invest many hours of sweat equity labor in their own futures. Former President Jimmy Carter and (wife) former First Lady Rosalynn have become integral working partners in HFH, yearly participating in the actual construction of a large number of homes. The philosophy of HFH is that which I espouse: creating situations in which average community members can engage in socially responsible, self-fulfilling, cooperative enterprise—the totality of effort engendering attitudinal and societal change.

But two questions remain: 1) Would the building of even 10,000 homes in the $50,000 price range in Southern California answer the needs of those who receive approximately $320 a month from public assistance? and 2) Are we really avoiding a discussion of the reasons why people are homeless, and in particular, why women are increasingly becoming the largest *hidden*-homeless population?

Providing "affordable housing" is a necessity. It solves a problem for the working poor who have an economic base. But what happens if they lose that base? Again, they will become homeless. So, we must view affordable housing as just one aspect of a multi-faceted societal problem regarding the causes of and solutions to homelessness.

The servant-leader model proposed in this book addresses the broader issues. The concept was generated by field work conducted (in unequal proportions) in Maine, Maryland, Virginia, Washington, D.C., Pennsylvania, West Virginia, Delaware, New Mexico, and California. The personal experiences presented, then, are just a spit in the ocean. . . .

Chapter One

Hide-and-Seek Shelter and Sustenance

In 1971 I met an elderly woman who was washing her lingerie in the ladies room of a Baltimore hotel. While soaping, rinsing and blow-drying, she repeatedly and softly sang several lines. I only remember the last two: "You're on the run, or lookin' for fun; you need someone, I'm followin' the sun." I assumed she was a guest in the hotel and asked if something was wrong with the sink in her room. She scrutinized me—and then grinned. "I don't stay in hotels, dear. I just wash in them." We talked for over an hour and I discovered that she was homeless as a result of widowhood and poverty. She lived in a van and had been doing as the song said: following the sun from Massachusetts to Florida—and back again—for years. That healthy-looking, feisty and articulate lady did not fit my image of a poor homeless woman. Instinctively I knew not to offer any assistance or money as we waved goodbye. She would have been offended.

My acquaintance had tarried (in her van) for varying amounts of time in many cities, towns, and rural areas, and expressed strong opinions regarding the merits of staying uptown as opposed to downtown, on farmland rather than in milltowns, and along the coast in preference to inland stretches. When I began to pursue research pertaining to homelessness I recalled what had been emphasized: unless one is immobilized, even homeless women have options; one may elect to live among those with whom one once shared a lifestyle, or become an isolate, or choose to live wherever

1

one feels safe. With that in mind, I have always noted where a woman has been seeking shelter and listened for clues to where a woman would like to be if she could just manage to get to, say, the Midwest, or Louisiana, or New Hampshire. Sometimes that is the only assistance a woman needs to "get back on her feet," for there may be friends to provide housing, employment opportunities, or simply the peace of mind which is necessary to attend to practical matters.

1. Uptown

"Uptown" denotes that part of the city which is not only geographically opposite from downtown, but is differentiated by social demography. In other words, uptown refers to the costliest homes, the best grocers and restaurants, the poshest shops, and the most discriminating of private clubs as well as the individuals who thus occupy, select, purchase, and belong. Uptown implies residents' superior educational, social, professional, and/or economic status. Contrary to popular thought, many homeless women were once part of the uptown demography—and they survive in the state of homelessness only because they imitate the way they once lived. They also call upon their ingenuity to satisfy old habits by technological and psychological practices.

Retrofitting a Car, Re-training Foodways, and Re-marriage

Sondra (age 56, Pacific Palisades, California, 1986) explains how she has managed to continue living in an exclusive area on an income of $325 a month:

> When Herb decided he wanted a divorce, he was prepared. All of our assets were channeled into accounts I couldn't touch—in fact, I didn't even know where they were. I just knew we had property and money. And stocks, of course, and a lot of jewelry that he had bought for investment purposes. You know, like diamonds and emeralds. Loose ones . . . gemstones. . . .

My lawyer was pretty much of a wimp and didn't have the wits to go after what we both knew was there for me. But maybe he has the wits and just figured I was an easy five thousand bucks and had better cases to pursue. Who knows. Anyway, I got suckered into signing a paper which said that I'd pretty much get what Herb acknowledged. And boy, did he ever seem to have Alzheimer's. "What do you mean, we have gems and property," he'd say in stunned amazement, and soon the judge agreed the poor guy was practically broke. So I was damn lucky to get $325 a month. . . . And when the house was sold I knew I'd only get a few thousand because Herb mortgaged it to the hilt. So there I was with about $15,000 to my name and nowhere to go where that wouldn't be eaten up within two years.

I had a fancy new Caddy, fortunately, and it was paid for. I sold some really good clothing and put that money right into outfitting the car. Like a bar attachment—with water, you know—and an empty back—no seat—but with a rod for hanging clothing. And drawers under a futon. Oh, I kept an old mink coat. It's a great blanket—and a bed cover. I put in tinted windows so no one can see inside, so I have my privacy. So I've got a place to live, and I couldn't rent anything as good. [She paused to think for a minute.] There's more to it than that. I would be raving insane in a crummy area, maybe in a one-room hovel. I'd rather be dead. So I'm living in the only way I can to keep my sanity. . . .

I did try to get a job, but you know, I'd been a homemaker and volunteer for so many years that no one would even consider hiring me. I majored in art history and philosophy, and I can tell you with authority that there isn't anything out there for over-fifty-years-old women with no experience. I did take a department store job last Christmas season, and I couldn't learn to use those new machines. What ever happened to cash registers? Not that I know how to work one, but I wouldn't have had an anxiety attack right there on the floor!. . . .

I'm lucky in that I found a place to park my car and not be towed away. The only old friend I had who still speaks to me. . . has some land abutting her property and it isn't used except for her satellite dish. I keep my car there when I'm not going the short distances to shopping centers or wherever I want within my budget for gas. I can pay for registration fees but not for car insurance, and if I get caught in an accident I'm in really big trouble. I'm ultra-careful about driving and avoiding traffic. . . .

I've had to re-train myself about food. I used to keep a healthy larder and wine cellar, and I ate at all times of the day. Now I've learned how to eat less and buy things that I can stretch for several days. It's funny, I guess, but if you keep thinking along the lines of wine and gourmet foods, you can eat less and yet feel fulfilled. I don't know where the term "dirty rice" comes from, but I make my own from a combination of a quart of plain rice from a Chinese carry-out, sprouts—they stretch any recipe—and mashed beans from a Mexican carry-out, canned peas and onions, and a fun variety of Trader Joe's cheapest wines. It keeps well in a box I've devised that's insulated for cooling, and I take some every night to a place with a microwave and have that with some cheap but good side dishes. A huge, gooey cinnamon bun with coffee in the late morning makes a brunch. About two I eat vegetables and fruit—usually apples, oranges, bananas, carrots, and cucs—but it depends on what's cheap and in season.

I have an early dinner—about five—and then I have a couple of glasses of red wine with a big slice of cake or my favorite peanut butter cookies from a gourmet store around eight while I watch TV. Oh, I took a very good portable TV from my husband's office before he noticed it was gone. . . . I've learned how to keep things warm on the little candle-lit things that are supposed to cook potpourri to make your room smell good, and all in all, I can manage on the $325 as long as I don't become ill. That's the big fear I have. What happens if I have to go to a doctor? I guess I'll have to pull a Scarlett on that one. . . .

I don't know how long I can last like this, but I try to go to places where I can meet nice men, and I hope that I can remarry. I'd marry almost anyone who I know could take care of me. That's not very nice, is it? But it's a necessity if I'm going to live. I go to Sunday services at alternating Beverly Hills, Pali, and Brentwood churches, and I stick around as long as I can. And I go to every wedding I can at those churches hoping that I'll meet someone. I try to avoid becoming friendly with the women because I know if just one finds out about how I'm living, everyone will know in an hour, and that will be the end of finding a man. I just don't know what else to do. . . .

Obviously I try to stay as nice-looking as I can, and I had to cut my long hair so I can wash it easily in [a hotel] ladies room and keep it looking as if I still go to the beauty parlor. A good cut every three months does that. And I keep my nails beautiful. I think that really marks the well-kept woman. Showers are a luxury, and I go to three hotels during a week to find rooms which have just been vacated, and I sneak in and use the bathroom and their shampoos and free goodies. That really means early in the morning or late in the afternoon. It's a chore, but it's worth it. . .

And it's a good thing I found out about the handicapped card for my car dashboard; I don't have to worry about paying for meters.

Dignity by Charting the Day's Activities

Grace (age 62, West Los Angeles, California, 1984) is also living in the neighborhood in which she was once a property owner. She manages to remain in control of her homeless situation by following a routine of daily activities which signify a sense of dignity:

Now look, it's really not *that* bad for me [being homeless in West Los Angeles]. I'd rather have my old life back, and that's a fact, but since Hank died and I used up our savings, I've had to improvise. We lived close to here and I know a lot of these storekeepers from the days when I was in and out with money. Well now, I haven't told them I've found a garage that is going to be unused for some time to come, and that's where I'm sleeping for the time being. I don't go back to the few that knew my address, and the others won't know....

There was an old daybed left that I fixed up with material given to me by a fabric store that was going out of business, and some terrible tables and outdoor chairs that I've had plenty of time to repair with odds and ends picked up in alleys along these great streets.

I'd go mad if I couldn't stay in this or any other really good neighborhood, so I managed to figure out how to arrange that. I've got this big paper on my wall with my days charted out. I'm pretending to be just like I was, and some days I go wandering through the department stores and then sit for a couple of hours with coffee and magazines in their eating places. One week I'll go to the department stores, and then the next I'll go through the little shops along Wilshire and San Vicente. There's lots of little places to eat along those streets. Then for a treat I'll go into Westwood and rob a bank. No! Just kidding! What I do is take my little pension check and go to the bank there, and get it all in ones. That makes me feel like I have a lot of money, and it looks good to the waitresses and waiters when I take out my wallet to pay for coffee and croissants at one of the restaurants where I can stay without being hassled. My, how the help has changed since I was young. Now everyone is rude and tries to pull you in and push you out so fast! Sometimes the young ones feel sorry for me, but the older waitresses have no patience at all....

So I go strictly by my chart and spend every day as if I were normal, and I don't think anyone suspects that I'm really homeless. I couldn't rent a room in Watts for what I have a month, and I don't know what will happen when that garage is gone. The house that it belongs to is owned by an elderly couple. They have a maid who doesn't do much anymore, and going out back is one. It hasn't been used in years. The maid parks the car in the front drive after she goes shopping. And since a pool and trees separate the house from the garage, there really isn't anyone to see me. I go in and out by the alley, and no neighbors use it except to take their cars in and out. So I just watch carefully when I come and go. If I hadn't lived so near, I never would have noticed the garage. I just got lucky.

I couldn't just stay in the garage, though. That's just for nights. I have to spend my days going from one food place to another, getting a little something here and a little something there in-between stalking the stores. It's enough to keep me busy and thinking about what I'll do when the owners die and the place is up for sale. . . .

I'm planning. . . by now I know a bit about how to fend for myself. Not enough, and not like what I was used to. I need some basics and a way to get around. The ideal would be a motor home [she laughed], but that would cost as much as a house—well, in a lousy section, maybe—and I can't see how that's in my future. Unless I could share with someone. That's really what I'm looking for, if you want the God's honest. I'm keeping my eye out for a widow with enough to get the motor home and needs someone to go along—for the ride, maybe, like as a friend, or needs help. I read bulletin boards and newspapers and listen in on conversations at senior center meetings. I'm not alone. . . I'll solve this.

Contracting the Future

Marian (age 57, Lancaster, Pennsylvania, 1979) has the motor home but does not wish to share it or travel.

Naw, this tub ain't one of your travelers. I don't go nowhere. I ain't got money for that. This is where I live now. When I got evicted—that old bum, Stringer, wanted to double our rents—I found this left by folks that came as tourists and left to get a divorce. They just left it on the land back of the restaurant after a whopping fight that people still talk about. I was looking for food at the kitchen door when I saw the cops looking it over. I asked what they was going to do with it, and the one just laughed. So instead of letting him have it, I paid one of our local hoodlets—that's them that are too young to be hoodlums—two bucks to hotwire it and I just toodled down the road to a lady friend's store. When she sold out, she told the new owners that I was to stay here, and it's in the contract. I got ninety-nine years. . . .

I'm in a terrific neighborhood—better than where I was renting—and if I wasn't so busted, I'd get new plumbing and fill the tank. Can't do much with a rusted old tub like this, but it's better than the basement at the college. That's where I thought I'd end up. . . .

A Stable Environment

A vehicle does not have to be in running condition for a homeless woman to take advantage of the varied opportunities afforded by the best areas. Randy (age 44, Los Angeles, California, 1986) lives in her car in a section of hillside homes: large, off-the-street, and mostly gated.

This damn old thing just won't start. It still looks pretty good, though, huh? I got it cheap with what I won in Vegas a couple of years ago, and it was the best thing I ever bought. I never thought I'd be on the streets in a few months, and it means I don't have to go to no lousy neighborhood to live. I can stay right here until the car rusts through. . . .

Every once in a while the private cops take a flashlight at me, but no real cops come up this way. They figure these people got electrified gates and alarms, so why cruise these hilly

streets? It's a blessing for me. I just pulled into this turn-
around and stayed. The people who live on this street just
whiz on past. They're so snooty, I guess they think this
belongs to one of the help. You know, don't let the maid or
butler park on the grounds 'cause their car don't look so
good!

I can walk the mile to the main street and then on to the
stores. You gave your word of honor not to tell what I do, so
I'm telling you I just take things I need. I got a radio with
batteries that I keep on a lot, and if I can cop a small bat-
teried TV, I will. I took a purse from a dressing room in a
fancy shop that keeps me going when I just have to use
money. I'll do it again when I run out. [She was very
defiant.] If I'm supposed to feel guilty about stealing, then
all the oil companies and insurance company executives better watch out for the Devil himself. I pick up the
newspapers. There isn't hardly anyone in Washington who
isn't a crook. No one really cares. At least, I don't see the
biggest crooks going to jail. . . .

Thanks for the bags of cookies, but I can get better ones at
the store down the hill. Give them to someone who hasn't
got the guts to take care of herself.

Safety in the Right Kind of Numbers

Martha (age 57, Herndon, Virginia, 1979) decided that large numbers of people living in an exclusive neighborhood were synony-
mous with safety.

This is a nutty way to live, but it's better than any of the alternatives I have. I get $265 a month to live on, and I can't
rent anything for that and have money for food and other
things. So when Tom wanted a divorce and had his partner
fix it so he only would have an income of $1000 a month—
and is that ever a lie since he can make that in the market
every week—I didn't have a chance for any new start in life.

We sold our house and damned if my name wasn't on the ownership papers. I know it was there when we bought the house together twelve years ago! I sold a few pieces of furniture and felt real lucky that my name was on the [car] pink slip. Tom would have grabbed that too if he could have. . . .

So one day I just packed up the car—at least it's a station wagon—and drove off. I had no idea where to go. It took weeks of just driving around before I figured I'd better get a new bank account and a post office box so my check could be sent to me. And then I knew I couldn't just keep driving and stopping. It wasn't safe at night on the street. And I was using all my money on gas. Then I was terrified that my car would break down in some awful place and I'd be stuck. So I drove into all the best neighborhoods and found the streets with privacy where I could park all night. I stay for as long as I can in one area without getting the attention of the patrol cars, and then I just move a few blocks away. Sometimes I park in the lot of an all-night grocery store if I feel scared, but it's hard to sleep with all those lights. The best places are where the high-rise condos are. A lot of people park there and it's pretty safe. I feel safe watching all those fur capes and alligator shoes going past the doormen who spend their days just watching for suspicious men who might rob their big tippers.

Plotting Anonymity While Retaining Individuality

A van is more spacious than a car and offers its occupant the opportunity to create a personalized interior. Jeannine (age 52, Towson, Maryland, 1978) is proud of her van but notes a problem and solution attendant to van living in an area of expensive homes:

It's not bad, huh? I got it fixed up and I can cook on my own little stove. See? [She showed me her innovative stove made from a cut-down barbeque unit.] I open this window when I'm cooking, and there's not too much smoke inside. That there's the bathroom. [She pulled me to the rear of the van where she had curtained-off a makeshift toilet and washbowl. The toilet was a bucket painted with flowers, and the washbowl looked to be an antique from the 1800s. She said she "picked it up at a flea market sale."] I have my living room right where the two chairs are, and instead of an "L" dining room, I got an "I." That table right in front is my dining room. And I got pictures on the walls, and curtains. . . I made those; nice, huh?. . . .

I'm proud of what I got and I'm proud of being smart enough to stay on good streets. Lotsa women I know park their cars and vans on bad side streets with lots of drug trafficking going on right beside 'em. I can't figure them out. . . . I got it fixed so's I can stay as long as I want on good safe streets, if there's such a thing anymore. But I been bothered by some of the residents 'cause the van sticks out. Cars, now, aren't so obvious. So what I did was drive slowly 'round in the evening at dinnertime and right about breakfast and see which houses have teenaged boys who have vans. Then I park right near those houses and apartments, and the neighbors think my van belongs to one of their friends. I stay for a couple a days on one street and move to another, and come back again. You see, if the neighbors see the same van come back again and again, they don't get worried that it's a burglar. I park only when I know I'm in for the night, so no one sees I'm a lady. The van's got to look right, and so's the driver. You got to fit, wherever you are, and part of that's the van, and part of it's me as a person.

Medical Complexes and Personal Appearance

Looking one's (appropriate) best is extremely important, for almost all of the women recognize that anonymity protects their continued presence. Carol (age 49, Westwood, California) told me (in 1985) how she had been living in a large medical school complex (in a fashionable area) for almost two years.

There are so many buildings and floors that I got lost the first few months. But I figured out how to keep moving from one wing and floor to another, and how long I could pretend to be visiting someone in the hospital ward sections without making anyone suspicious. I can pick up good snacks in any of the canteen corners; someone always leaves something good during the day because they are upset or in a hurry. The cafeterias are good because food is left on the tables and I just move on in before someone takes the trays away. . . .

The bathrooms have soap and body cream, so I take a sponge bath every day. I keep my hair neat and change styles when I move back into a section that I've been in recently. Maybe put on glasses, too. And wear a skirt instead of slacks. I try to change my appearance. . . .

The sofas in the waiting rooms are soft. No one notices if I go to sleep. Most visitors do in some sections, anyway, because a patient may be in X-Ray, or surgery, or just taking a nap. Everyone leaves magazines and newspapers around, and the place is open all day and night.

I won't say this is a good way to live, but it's safe and better than a mission or roaming the streets. You know, I shouldn't say this, but I visit with some of the older patients sometimes, you know, in the orthopedic or recovery wards when I'm walking up and down the long hallways and see the lonely ones with no visitors. Every once in a while I'll let on that I'm in bad shape financially when I can tell that it's a person with money, and I've been given money and asked to come back and visit again. I'm saving a little money now— enough to have a small bank account—and maybe when I meet a nice woman or man who likes my company, maybe they'll ask me to come and share a home with them. I keep looking for what I once had, but I know that can't be and so I'll have to work it out another way. . . and some nice lady or gent is going to get a good companion in me.

I think after so long that some nurses and doctors probably know what I'm doing, but they haven't snitched yet. I don't really bother anyone, and I do help the lonely people. And listen, this is a good place to be. If I get sick, I'm in with the right people!

Mall Life

Sherry (age 54, West Los Angeles, California, 1988) exemplifies those women who are spending more and more time in malls. Many malls are being built in the very best sections of town, and older women in particular—regardless of economic circumstances—find themselves beginning the day by walking through stores and ending the day by taking groceries home from the mall-attached markets. In Sherry's case, of course, she has no home to which to return. However, as mall life becomes a morning 'til nighttime experience, who is to tell who is simply lonely at home and who is homeless?

> I guess that no one really knows that I haven't got any place to go but where I am at any time. I got all my necessaries in these nice big bags with Bullock's, Broadway, and Nordstrom on them. It's a heavy load to schlep around, but it's better than not having anything I can call my own, like some I know. . . .

> I used to be one of the crowd; you know, shopping, eating out and going to movies. That's pretty much what I do now. Just in a different way. . . for free. And it's not all that hard, except that I'm always afraid that I'll be discovered—you know, that I'm bumming my way through life—and put in jail for being a transient, or maybe for stealing. I have to do that for a lot of my food. I eat fruit and cheese and crackers in the grocery stores, but I'm not the only one. Regular people do it all the time. They call it "tasting." So no one really notices when I'm walking along with a half-filled grocery cart and eating an apple out of my bag of apples, or that I've opened one of my boxes of cookies. I call that strollin'-'n-eatin'. Those gourmet hot food counters are great for chicken and big fried potatoes. You just order what you want and then eat it slowly before you get to the pay counter. I know it's stealing, but I'm not about to starve

myself or live like a beggar in a poor area when there are terrific neighborhoods where I can live kind of like I used to. Before the bum stole our life savings and took off with his twenty-two year old twinkie. To Mexico yet, where he always promised me we'd go together after he had it made. Anyway, here are the things I was used to, and I'm not so dumb I'm going to move to the slums just because I'm poor. Hell, poor! I'm broke and trying to exist! So unless some miracle happens, and maybe it will since I buy a lottery ticket every week, I'm hanging in there with the rich....

I spend my time in three nice malls. But to make it work you got to have bags with the mall store names on them. Otherwise you don't fit in. I know a real dumb gal who uses Saks bags where there ain't no Saks, and she's a stand-out. And a couple of ladies stay in one mall, and that's dumb 'cause the guards begin to notice you. I move around so that I don't stand out as too much of a regular. . . I never stay on one level for long, and never two days in a row. And Lordy, I don't fall asleep on the mall benches. And I'm pretending to use the telephone before I start to check the slots for loose change. . . . If I play my cards right, no one will figure that I'm anything but a bored housewife with nothing much to do but shop around all day.

Changing Environments and "The Restaurant Scam"

While Sherry focuses on mall-life for her existence, other women prefer an alternating routine. Stephanie (age 56, Santa Monica, California) said in 1986:

I start with a library where I can relax in a comfy chair and read up on all the news or just enjoy a good mystery novel. I do that at least three days a week, sometimes in Santa Monica and sometimes in Beverly Hills, and people just think I don't have too much to do at home—maybe have the empty nest syndrome. Then I'll go to one of the two malls nearby and clean myself up in the fancy ladies rooms. One has two rooms, one just like a living room—with better sofas than I ever had at home. I can take a long nap twice a day, but I make sure I'm upright. I never lie down. Rich people notice that. I can be a tired shopper, but not a vagrant using the couch. It's okay, though, because a couple maybe three long naps up against the cushions adds up to a night's sleep. . . . Nights? Well, I do a lot of sitting in twenty-four hour coffee shops and riding on buses. It's only from 2 a.m. 'til 6 that it's tough. As soon as it's light I start to walk to the library and wait on the side—where the employees can't see me when they come in. I sit on the grass with coffee and donuts and a book.

I've never had to go hungry for long. I moved from a small town to Cleveland to L.A., and what you can't do in a town is what keeps me alive in a big city. There are lots of decent restaurants, and I figured out how to get some real good meals. You really only need three of those a week, you know, and the rest of the time you can snack anywhere. I got this restaurant scheme going. I look around for a couple of women having lunch or dinner together, and wait until they're almost finished. Then I pass by them on my way to the ladies room.

I lean over and look like I'm about to join them, and am chatting. What I do is ask if one of them is Ann Roman, 'cause I'm supposed to be meeting a new friend there. Of course the women are usually polite and talk for a sec, and I sort of wave and go off to the ladies room. When they leave, I slip into their booth or table real fast, and signal for their waitress. I explain that I was late and my friends had to leave, but they'll be back in a bit for coffee with me since we're going to a movie, but I'm famished, and I order. No one is suspicious, and I eat a good meal. Then I have two choices. I can either pull out my credit card—which is an out-dated one I found in the trash—and become shocked that I haven't replaced it with my new one, so I'll have to wait for my friends to come back and loan me money, or if I'm lucky, there's a back door—usually it's through the kitchen—that I can use. If I'm waiting for my friends, I just inch toward the door, looking for them, and then finally go outside to look down the street—and disappear. You don't go back to the same restaurants unless you know exactly who is on duty and when the managers change shifts, so you need a big city!

Happy Hours for Free Food

Gwen (age 47, Santa Monica, California, 1987) found that "happy hours" are popular in all parts of town, but that the quality and variety of foods in the higher-priced restaurants is worth living in the areas which support several "happy hour" restaurants.

I guessed a year ago that if I was going to make it on the streets, I'd have to be where there was good, free food. You can always bedroll-down in some park or city property. I did my share of eating in the stores, but I knew I'd have to find an area of, oh, maybe five miles, where there'd be a group of restaurants that had really good happy hours. When I found the Marina and Santa Monica, I just knew I'd be here for a long time!....

The only way to go wrong is to go back too many times in a row to the same place, unless you can afford to buy drinks, of course. That makes it all okay. But I just get a lemonade or iced tea and lots of ice to spread it out for maybe two hours while I eat. And I'm careful to look like I'm just nibbling and don't really want the food. At first I pretended I was waiting for a friend, especially at the Marina where you get noticed in a nice restaurant—the waitresses stay for longer and get to recognize you—but then I saw other singles and figured I didn't have to be ashamed to be alone . . . .

I have a sort of route that I follow, from the Main Street to the Marina restaurants, and there are enough of them so that I can get fresh vegetables and fruits, and chicken made every way you can think of, to lobster and crab in some places, to sandwiches and desserts. As long as you keep a drink in front of you, it's fine. I spend a lot of time getting that money together, for that's my means of getting free food every day. . . I need about two bucks a day, and mostly I can find that on the beach. . . mostly in the parking lots and in the ladies rooms. But I just sort of follow the drunks. They sure do know where to find loose change!

I spend every evening in a nice restaurant where it's pleasant and safe. I guess that's as much as I can expect out of life now. With my business gone and all—that's what happens when you go bankrupt and suddenly find yourself out of the chips—I don't think in terms of miracles. It's me and some nice clothes just wandering. But I'll be damned if I'm going to spend my last years where it isn't safe and pleasant.

From the Car to the Temple

Vicky (age 63, Los Angeles, California, 1986) has a similar idea regarding her environment, but relates it to her particular background:

When Sam died and I was so lonely, I used to just go to temple to sit and have someplace that made me feel like I still belonged to someone—whether it's God or just the surroundings where I used to go be with Sam, I don't know— but being alone wasn't quite so horrible in the temple. Then when I couldn't make the house payments and moved into an apartment, I really couldn't stand the little place and I went to the temple for space. . . .

When my savings account read in the hundreds, I knew I'd have to re-think my future—such as it is. The most money I was spending was on food—after the rent, that is. The rent problem I solved by selling all my furniture and taking the money and putting it into a better car so I could sleep there. And don't ask me how I managed to do that without going crazy, please. I just did what I had to do. There wasn't any choice; I tried all the regular channels for getting aid, and nothing was enough for a spaniel to get a good dog house. . . .

The temples always have a good spread on Fridays and holidays, and then there are all the special days, too, from meetings to wedding receptions. I went to the rabbi and asked for charity to join, and I'm there all the time. On Friday nights after services, I eat like a pig and take things home—did you hear that? Home! Back to the car! So, that's how it is. . . . I do the same thing every time there's an event. And then I started to go to some of the other temples and now I go to four and stock up on food. It's also a change of scenery for the daytime hours.

The Meaning of "Church" and a Grocery Store

Ruthie (age 73, Los Angeles, California) spends as much time as she can in churches. In 1984 she had already made herself known in practically every church in the better neighborhoods of Los Angeles as "that praying woman."

I got more beads and religious items than a Christian store. I use them churches just like Jesus would want everyone else to. If God meant for churches to be built, He meant for them to be used. So why shouldn't I? The ones who keep saying they're so religious don't go except on a Sunday when some-one makes them go. I got a mat that I put down on a pew to make it more comfortable, and I can take a snooze or sit in peace and read or knit or write in my book. Poetry. That's what I write. When the book is full of just the right poems, I'll try to get it published. . . .

I think it's pretty bad when they tell you to get out because it's closing time. What do they think churches are, bars? God would want them open all day and all night! Well, I tell them preachers—I call all of them preachers whether they want to be called that or not, 'cuz they're just preaching God's word and it's not like they're something special in-stead of being God's servants—what God would say about putting people out on the streets from church. But one o' them preachers found a place where I can spend nights safely. I won't tell you where. I got a right to my privacy. [A nun told me that she is allowed to stay in a small utility building attached to one of the churches. It has a cot and running water.]

I got this good relationship with St. Anne. I tell her what I feel and she listens real good. She has to. She's stone. But every once in a while I feel like she's staring at me—when I'm not sitting where she should be staring at me. Maybe her spirit and what's left of mine get together in those empty halls and mix it up. I don't want you thinking I'm nuts, but I get these times when I hear us both talking to each other. . . . It's just the nerves playing tricks on an old woman. . . . This is Hell, you know. I been skinflinted. Hell is here. . . .

You want to know where I get food? Where does anyone get it? In a grocery store! I fill up my cart and eat some things out of it twice a day. It's no big deal to just leave the basket in an aisle and wander off. Sometimes I get in the under-ten-items line with a jar of something I can't eat there . . . Do you know how much money I used to give to those stores when I had my own home? Enough extra in their profits to make up for the little I eat now. Nasty rich kids open boxes and take candy, cookies, and chips all the time, anyway. You ever see a mother scold one?

Abandoned Homes

Another manner of isolating oneself in an upper-class area is to utilize a home which has been closed by the owner—and is far enough away from neighbors to allow the homeless person to dwell undetected. Selma (age 59, Bel Air, California, 1987) only became publicly known because she reported a mugging, tried to retract her statement, and was referred to me because it was thought she might be the victim of abuse by a family member.

This is just *awful*! I don't know why I didn't just ignore the letters. It's all because I can't find a job. I'm just too old to be hired anymore, and I don't know where to go! I'm trusting you not to give me away. Remember, it's on your head if I end up dead on the street tomorrow!. . . .

I used to work for the Browns [pseudonym] and was given a month's notice before they announced a divorce and went their separate ways. The house was to be renovated and put up for sale. No one was supposed to come in before it was shown except the contractors, and I knew I had a couple of weeks before they came. I know because I heard them talking about all of this, so I felt pretty safe about what I did. . . .

I couldn't find another job, so I hung around the house and watched the Browns move out. They couldn't leave fast enough, and even though I gave them back my keys, I had had one made up that let me in the garden entrance that had another door that went straight into the atrium—and then into the kitchen. I waited until that night and just went in like I had done for eight years.

All the utilities was turned off, and I was careful to keep the drapes closed that was left up. I kept waiting for the decorators and a building crew, but they never showed up. Then I read a letter which was supposed to be sent on to Mrs. Brown but was put in the mail slot. All the original plans were put on hold because something wasn't signed, and she was supposed to get in touch with the lawyer right away.

I thought I had it made, and settled right in. I kept trying the agencies, but no one even wanted to interview me. Time just sort of went by, and I used up all of the money I had for food. The Browns gave me cash so's they wouldn't ever have to pay any taxes, and I found out that that meant I'd have no benefits. Too bad I didn't know that for eight years. Shouldn't they have to tell an employee? Well, I guess not.

I'm not supposed to be stupid. I should have known to ask about it. . . .

I got to taking a few things from the grocery store, and that got to be a habit, so I ate okay. It was so easy. And I wasn't hurting anyone. I can't be arrested for that now, can I?

One day someone I guess was a lawyer came to the house and walked through, making notes. I hid in the kitchen closet and watched him. I almost had a heart attack wondering if he would notice what I'd arranged for myself, but he didn't see nothing wrong. Then he locked-up the house and went away, and it's been seven months since anyone has come around here. Oh, the gardener comes every Thursday, but he does his thing and moves along fast. [She laughed.] He goes much faster than when there was the lady of the house watching that he was doing all the work. . . .

So, there isn't much in the way of furniture, just some stuff they didn't want. There were some blankets and towels left—not the good ones, of course—and some clothes, both men's and women's, supposed to be given to Goodwill. I made myself a bedroll and stuffed a lot of clothes into a chair with a broken seat. [She laughed.] They were in such a rush, they just left lots of soap and toothpaste and things that they didn't need but I do. They left a lot of earthquake survival stuff, too. You know, everything from bottled water to tins of sardines. If they'd kept me on 'til the very end, they'd have made me throw it all away. But they were too cheap and in a hurry to get on with their own good times. . . .

I know this can't last, and I was really dumb to report the mugging. But I was taken to have some stitches in my hand and a doctor at the emergency room saw bruises on my forehead—they were from tripping on my own feet and falling against the wall—and the cop put that in the report. I gave the Brown's address and never thought anyone would follow up. But when no one answered the phone, letters started coming. I figured it would be smart to just call and say I was okay and no one I knew hurt me, and look what happened. Here I am, trying to make everyone leave me alone, and now someone thinks that I'm in trouble with a family person who's beating on me. So can't you just put down it's all a big, stupid mistake and I didn't know the guy who really did mug me? I don't. He was just a mugger. . . .

It would be so much easier if someone would just help me get another housekeeping job. If the utilities were on, I'd take the chance of using the kitchen and charging stuff at [the gourmet grocery store] where the Browns always did. I could just say I'd been kept on to take care of the house. That's believable. And I'd make my super choco-coffee cake and peddle it to [a local bakery]. I could make a living off of my desserts.

I lived in Austria and Switzerland when I was younger, and I learned to feed my sweet tooth. I know just how to use chocolate. Most people think there's just milk and dark, but there's lots of kinds of chocolate, and you got to use just the right one for a special taste. Now my favorite is the bitter chocolate melted and mixed evenly with amaretto coffee to make a paste before you fold in pure cream—you know what I mean by pure cream? Americans think that awful stuff, uh, half and half, is cream—and then I add vanilla bean. . .[pause] but if I tell you the recipe, it won't be mine anymore, will it? But it don't really matter. I don't know how I'd get the desserts to bakeries without a car. You can't be going without a car in L.A. if you want to do a business, and I'd like to try that.

Seasonal Homes, Natural Foods, and Solar Cooking

Isolation in an "uptown" area may also refer to the woman who finds a seasonal home to inhabit. These homes are often in coastal communities or in clusters around lakes, and are not necessarily "rural" despite the presence of wooded areas and water access or views; many year-round residents are active members of (small) city or town life which may include colleges, symphonies, and museums. An example comes to mind because I spent many months in just such an exclusive area in Maine. There are always houses vacant for both summer and winter seasons—the first because of changed vacation plans, and the latter because many cottages are not meant for cold-weather living (nor are their summer occupants). One summer when I did have a place to stay, I noted that a cottage situated on a tiny inlet nearby showed signs of habitation when I knew that the owners were in Europe for the season. Out of curiosity—and being foolish or innocent enough not to think of thieves--I investigated. I saw a curtain move. I saw garbage hidden behind the back steps which had been strewn in the night by some scavenging animal. I did not want to frighten the woman (and I knew it was a woman because of certain items in the trash), so I left a note under a stone by the back door saying I would return later to chat and that I had no intention of telling anyone that she was there. I found a woman not unlike myself who had found a safe haven for as long as it might be available. She had no knowledge of a time frame, so that each moment was spent wondering if the next would be the one in which she was discovered and punished.

I only use the living room because I do have some principles. I know that this house belongs to someone else, and I wouldn't be here if I had any alternatives. I tried to stay in my car, but it's too cold at night. And then it got towed away from the hotel parking lot. . . and I was hitching, not knowing where to go, and I just let the person take me too far down the peninsula. All I could do was walk around town and hope that I could find some place to sleep. Someone in the grocery store was gossiping about the people here not coming for the summer, and what a shame to waste such a beautiful place. It is, isn't it? It reminds me of the kind of home that is every person's dream, and I pretend that it is mine. . . .

So I walked for miles until I found the place, and then I had to figure out how to get here, because it seemed that the only way in was at low tide or by boat. I didn't want to steal a boat. Not because I'm so honest, but it would be obvious that it was gone and someone would see it from the ocean side. I found the land entrance, but I usually use the low tide so no one sees me. That doesn't give me much time to find food and get back. And I have to copy the paper to make sure I have the tide timetable right.

I've been here for two months now, and I hope they stay away all year. But you never know if they'll tell friends they can use the house, and I'll suddenly be faced with strangers staring at me and calling the police. I haven't broken anything except the pane in the basement window, and I fixed that right away so no one will notice. The water's pumped from a well, and no electricity is on, so I haven't spent any of their money. . . .

Winter will be awful, and I'm trying to decide how to tackle the cold, snow, and getting food. But I am going to try. Right now I'm cooking seafood—everything from mussels that I learned how to dig to fish I've caught with a rod I made from a tree branch—and potatoes and corn in a double wooden crate lined with tin foil and a glass top to reflect the sunlight. It's where the sun hits near noon for a few hours, but I don't know what to do come gray skies and snow!

I'll have to use the fireplace or the woodstove, but someone's bound to see the smoke. I am going to plan this carefully. I'm already watching all of the nice houses across the water to see if these are just summer people. . . .

I'm so frightened, but this is better than being forced in and out of missions. I'll never go to one of them again.

I make no excuse for "assisting" her in a sojourn in someone else's house. When I found that she was determined to stay, we had wonderful long discussions in which we strategized how she would get food, test the wind, and change living plans suddenly if necessary. I did do some scouting for Betty (age 47, Portland, Maine,

1978), and before I left in September she knew that she was facing summer cottages, and she had decided to use the woodstove for cooking and heat during the nighttime and only on days when no one would be likely to notice smoke drifting from the island. We talked about her future and my future, and I have always wondered how she fared. I left an address, hoping that she would write, but I have never heard from her. From what she told me that summer, I think it likely that she continued to live in closed seasonal homes. She would have been an expert after one full year.

Parks

The year-round good weather in Southern California has created an alarming increase in a "permanent" homeless population. In the Los Angeles area, reasonably safe parks are scattered throughout the cities which stretch from the Hollywood Hills to the airport and from near-downtown to the beaches. While police try to keep the homeless from overtaking the parks in the better areas, many individuals sneak in to sleep behind bushes and flower gardens—and inside large pieces of modernistic sculpture which may serve as a bed. Sylvie (age 46, Holmby Hills, California) has found that she fits in quite well with the crowd at a park in a neighborhood of expensive homes. During 1984 and 1985 I encountered her often on my way back and forth to UCLA.

> Oh, I don't kid myself. I know that some of the smarter women know I don't live in the neighborhood. But most probably think I'm somebody's poor relation that's come to stay with them and they don't want me in the house all day. So I go to this park and sit on my blanket and read and sleep. Then, like everyone else, I do my jogging around the park a couple of times. When the park empties at certain times of the day, I just go to where I've been watching the rich people throw away good food. The kids eat half a sandwich and toss the rest in the trash can. The grown-ups seem to all have the stomach of an ant; they bring food in fancy baskets and then barely taste it. They even wrap it

before they throw it away. The women all weigh about 90 lbs., and I know why. . . .

I don't talk to anyone, especially the kids or maids; it's safer for everyone to think I'm snobby than to have to answer questions. I've found a good safe place to live, and it smells nice with all the roses around. The bathrooms are okay, and there's hot and cold water. The rich women leave combs and make-up and the teenagers drop money. I watch the games that the men and women play all dressed-up in white outfits. They can spend hours on what looks like lawn bowling. All in all, it's kind of like being retired in Florida or Hawaii. Isn't what I do what people with lots of money do?

Campuses

Because I was often at UCLA from 1981 to 1986, I had many occasions to notice women who seem to be living on the campus, which is in one of the most exclusive sections of (uptown) Los Angeles. There may also be male campus dwellers, but men usually have a harder time blending into a middle-to-upper-class scenario. The major reason is that any man who is not "clean" is the object of suspicion; males need to shave (or maintain a shaped beard), have clean and untorn clothing, and act as if they belong in a particular milieu. Perhaps women are better at "pretending"; certainly they have an easier task in caring for their appearance (as they have noted themselves). In addition, any man who wanders an area between early morning and evening is conspicuous while women are assumed to be natural elements of the daylight scene.

The women who live on large campuses have access to many of the same amenities that students do. Pearl (age 53, Westwood, California) told me her stories during 1985.

I have acres of greenery to live in. There are so many buildings with so many private rooms where people only go once in a while—and I found two that I can sleep in all night—and all kinds of places to find lost money to use in the machines that work twenty-four hours a day. The trash cans have fresh food tossed before classes, clothing is left everywhere, and there are millions of books to be read. It is a dream world for the person who wants to learn, learn, learn. I can walk into any undergrad lecture hall with the students. They only know a few of their own anyway. No one knows whether I am working on a degree or doing research or just hanging out. There are plenty of older women about, and I figure if I plan my movements just right, there will be no reason for me to leave here for years. Then I'll just go to another beautiful big campus. I'm sort of looking forward to that! You know, it occurred to me that I might just apply for graduate school and financial aid and live forever doing this legally. . . .

Museums

Some museums are in uptown areas, but it is the size, type, and ambience which determine whether someone can actually spend many a month undetected as "homeless," using the space for more than dalliance or research. Carrie (age 50, Washington, D.C.) had practically lived in the Smithsonian complex for several months before we talked in 1978.

This place is just heaven. There isn't anything I could want to see or read about that isn't right here. The guards just smile and secretly think I'm a home-hater. I'm sure they don't suspect that I actually live here. The only time I have to leave the buildings is when they close, and then I go to an all-night coffee shop where one of the waitresses knows me now and doesn't make me leave. Finally I'll go into a hotel lobby or just sit and sleep on one of the benches along the river. It's safe enough because there are always people— probably mostly visitors—walking around D.C. There are parts that are always pretty lively, and I just pretend that I'm exhausted and nod off. I found that wearing a tourist outfit makes me less conspicuous, too. You know what a tourist outfit is, don't you? Nothing matches and it's either all wrinkled or brand new. And then you add a camera hanging from your neck and sunglasses. There are lots of advantages to being in a place that's hopping. No one notices you. . . .

Hotels

The ability to remain anonymous is not at once associated with hotel living, but in large cities there are hotels in which many individuals retain permanent residences but are seldom on site. In the uptown sections of Los Angeles, New York, and the District of Columbia it is quite common to find hotel rooms kept as "homes" which are rarely used. Fiona (age 43, Washington, D.C., 1978) moves between two hotels:

Mrs. [X] really lives in Paris, London, and Zurich. But she keeps her room here at the [hotel] for whenever she's in town for some fancy event. And Mrs. [X] lives in Dallas but has a permanent room at the [hotel]. I found out about both by accident from one of the maids who changed jobs. She knows both hotels and what goes on. Well, we was talking in the laundromat—that's where I was living, really—when she began to talk about these two lucky women. Then this idea came to me. What was happening to those rooms when no one was there? Nothing! Isabella was scared to let me see the rooms, but I talked her into letting me. She had the master key for one, and I stayed one night. The next day she was crying and said I'd be found and I'd tell that she let me in. . . .

I promised not to tell, and she went to a lot of trouble to keep tabs on when [Mrs. X] might come to town. That meant that Isabella had to make real good friends with a bellboy, but that turned out okay because they got engaged. I know she must have told him about me, but she hasn't said so. Anyway, they make sure that I know how to get out fast and Isabella cleans up right away. That's in the one hotel. . . .

I had to get a key for [the other hotel], and that wasn't easy. I thought and thought about that and then one day the answer came to me in a TV story. All I had to do was wait

for a really busy day and push my way into the crowd at the
desk and ask real nice for my key, which I knew was in the
box. I took it just long enough to open the door and unlock
it, and then I rushed right back to return it, saying I'd asked
for the wrong room number. So no one suspected that it
was gone. I wanted to have a copy made, but I'd already
found out that no one is going to copy a hotel key—at least
not anyone legit. I'd tried. Then I had to find a way to keep
the door unlocked for me but locked for everyone else. That
was terrible hard. I guess if you watch enough TV you can
learn how to do just about anything, but I never saw that
one. What I do is to stay in the room all day and keep the
door locked and make sure I'm quiet so no housekeeper
hears anything she shouldn't. I can keep the TV on real
quiet and use the bathroom. I just make sure there's no one
nearby when I flush or use the tap. The rooms on both sides
are regular hotel rooms with new people all the time, so I
don't worry about them, and I can use the bathroom at
night—and the TV. That's when I go out, too, and bring up
food and stuff. I go out by the back entrance with the staff; I
never go through the lobby. I got a maid's uniform to use if
I get scared like I do sometimes if I think someone notices
me too much. But I can let the door stay unlocked at night
'cause no one is going to come in from the staff. If a burglar
gets in, well, that could happen with me or not. Right? [I
agreed.]

I know that someday I might get caught, and I got my story
all ready. I just got off the train from New York and my
purse was stolen, and all I was doing was staying for a day
until I could get my kids to send money. No one is going to
put me in jail for that; the worse I'll get is a good chewing
out. This hotel [the one with the lady who lives in Europe] is
where I don't know anyone, and I just go by what Isabella
learns from her contacts with the other maids who are still
here. She tells me when they talk about Mrs. [X] returning,
and I just clean up real good and move to the other hotel. A

couple of times they've been in town together, but it's not usual. I've got my eye out for other rooms that are kept by certain people, and I'm going to be prepared to use their rooms too. I've got to find a place that'll make me a dupe key for hotels. I keep trying to get a job cleaning for hotels, 'cause then I can just stay in the empty rooms, but so far I haven't. There's no place I can put as an address or phone number where I can be found, so I have to just keep going and asking. I want to stay in a good area, though, 'cause that's where I can always get what I need for free. What the rich throw out!. . . .

I know that I'm lucky to look pretty good. People don't even think I might have no place to go. I just wish that some of the jobs I might get didn't insist on an address and references. I'm willing to work. People seem to put obstacles in my path. I really try. I wasn't in this spot until my boss made passes at me and I quit, and then I couldn't get anything else and everything just went downhill. I still can't believe I'm doing this. I'm a good person. I work hard. [She started to cry.] I worked overtime—and all I got for it was having "the grope" coming after me. If I knew I could have sued for that, I would have. I didn't know about that until I saw it on TV. But you can't get a job without references, and now I'm reduced to living like a bum. . . and there doesn't seem to be a way out once you hit bottom. For me getting a job cleaning in a hotel is degrading, but it's all I have hopes for now.

Casinos

Many hotels in casino-cities such as Las Vegas and Atlantic City are utilized by homeless women (and others) as permanent living places. Along "the strip" in both cities, the ambience is strictly "uptown," although there are certainly boundaries which define the best hotels from those of lesser status. If not evaluated as uptown hotels, some of these unusual, self-contained dwelling spaces will be assumed to be midtown—denoting the area which is the connecting link between uptown and downtown or "crosstown" from one side to the other.

Thelma (age 55, Las Vegas, Nevada, 1986) came to Hollywood to see if the "bright lights" were worth a change of residence. Discovering that Hollywood is not what she had seen in the movies, she was preparing to return to Las Vegas when I met her in the ladies room of the Ambassador Hotel in Los Angeles (1986) while I was attending a four-day conference. She was shocked that Los Angeles "closed down" at night and lacked any opportunities.

> Las Vegas makes me feel alive! There's no difference between night and day; nothing ever closes, and there's always something exciting going on. I get to hear free entertainment, get free food and drinks, and sack out in the plushest lobbies. Hell, half the people there look worse than I do, especially if they've just lost a wad. Some of what they lost I find on the floor beside their drinks or under their chairs or alongside the slots....
>
> I get good clothes there for nothing; women leave scarves, sweaters, and even purses and coats when they leave in a hurry. And men! Hey, so many come in drag and just leave their female clothes in the closets. . . I spot 'em, follow 'em, and wait for them to leave the hotel. Some leave everything and I take what I can fit or trade....
>
> Everyone there is homeless, sort of. It's a transient place where everyone is out of sync for a time. I am really the only one who's settled. I know what's going to happen every day, and I plan for bettering the situation. I thought Hollywood would be bettering myself. But boy, what a horror this place is. I'm going to bus back tomorrow and get back into the swing of life.

While Pearl (age 60, Atlantic City, 1979) was telling me a similar tale of enjoyable living I almost forgot for the moment that she was homeless:

Vegas is a desert. Too hot. Here I can *live*. And there's no difference between night and day if you stay in the casino. Oh, there's less people around at four in the morning, but I can just stay in the ladies room or up in a hallway so that I don't stand out as being seen every day. But lots of people who live in Atlantic City spend almost all of their time in the casino, so no one really knows whether I have a home or not. Besides, if I don't bother anyone, no one cares. . . .

I gamble every once in a while just to keep up the image. I find change in the slots and on the floor and wait until someone finally gives up in the wee hours, and it only takes a few pieces of change to get that jackpot. . . .

There is always free food around somewhere. If it was something ordered, it gets left if the person leaves in disgust or a happy daze. Every once in a while, when I'm really on the outs, I pick a room number where the people have just gone out, and order room service. I leave a note on the door asking that the tray be left by the door because I'm in the shower. I don't like to do that, because I'm not really crooked. But I don't want to faint from hunger and become the face on a front page, either!

This is almost ideal. The weather is great in the summer, and I can roam the Boardwalk all day. In the winter is when I spend almost all day and night in the casino.

2. Midtown

Playtowns

Midtown areas in which tourists provide the major source of income are such entertainment complexes as Disneyland (Anaheim, California). I only interviewed one homeless woman there—Doris (age 45, 1983)—but she assured me that she was not the only "permanent resident" of the many-acred facility.

I got in on a pass given to me months ago, and I ain't leavin' 'til someone makes me!

It's a good place to hide, you know? I can dress up in different outfits that I make out of what I find around—left by the tourists in the bathrooms and on the benches near the rides and in the eating places. I don't think anyone really looks at tourists, anyway. We all look alike. Stupid and gawkin'. So that's what I do when I think someone who works there is lookin' at me. But they get a change in kids workin' here, and I move around a lot. . . .

I really had to hide the first few days when the gates closed, but I found a spot in one of the "worlds." I sleep there and no one thinks to look for someone like me. Most likely the staff would be lookin' for teenagers who'd be doin' it for a lark, and they'd pick someplace dumb and then give themselves away by playin' around after closin' time. I'm *real* quiet. . . .

Food is always left around, so's I eat pretty good, and when the place closes, I know where to get leftovers. That's when I just lie back and enjoy myself: me and food and the pretty places they've made here. It's like a movie set that I pretend is real.

Tracktowns

Foxy (age 51, Baltimore, Maryland, 1979) also likes the crowded atmosphere, the noise and excitement, and the anonymity offered by an ever-changing population. She and several other homeless women live at racetracks, often following the circuit. Most racetracks are midtown/crosstown; they are not in the uptown sections, and not in the business or industrial downtown areas.

I didn't even like horses when I found myself here by accident. See, I'd been with this guy who said if he won, he'd buy me dinner and—well—I knew I'd stay with him in a motel for the night. That's one night with a roof over my head. . . . I'd been sleeping behind the Reisterstown mall. . . .

When he didn't win and tried to get me to go off with him to some rathole, I decided to just make an excuse to use the bathroom—and never come out. Eventually he went away, and when the track closed for the night, I hid under the bleachers. I figured I'd be found, but when I wasn't, I spent the next day really hunting for a place or two where no one went at night and in the early morning. . . .

I really got a thing for the nags now. I can pick 'em better than most handicappers, and I get staked to bettin' by finding lost money or tossed winning tickets. When someone gets annoyed or thinks they've lost, they just toss their tickets on the ground. Lots of time the people are so drunk they don't know whether they've got a winner or not. And the really bad drunks just drop dollar bills after they leave the pay windows. I follow 'em.

I get enough to buy hot dogs and sodas, and there's always the food thrown away when someone gets angry or runs off to collect. I'm right there, waitin' for all those losers. . . .

It's easy to follow the racin' season if you want. You just go from one track to another along the route that the horses do, and soon you get to know all the horses that go up and down the coast. When you know them, you know which horse is just passin' through from New York to Florida and is put down in class to pay his expenses and which are moved up in class to test him. I just bet the best horse to show, and I'm almost always in the money. Not a lot, but enough to get by. . . . Every once in a while I'll take a flyer on a daily double—and every once in a while I get lucky. You got to watch them nags in the paddock, though. Just one case of the runny-trots and you figure he's goin' to bolt. A waste of money. . . unless you know he always gets nervous.

Beachtowns

Aggie (age 59, Ocean City, Maryland, 1979) exemplifies women who like a modicum of excitement and manage to live self-sufficiently in beachtowns. These sometimes-seasonal areas provide various amenities and opportunities which homeless women are able to plot for maximum security and obscurity.

I been up to Orchard Beach and all along the Massachusetts beachtowns down to all the Florida beaches. I kind of like the Cape because of the people and I guess I'll go back there next year. Right now it's good here 'cause they're building condos and I can stay in the ones being built or not lived in yet. . . .

It's the best living I've ever had, even when I was married and the hubby took me for a weekend trip to these places. Now I know how to get food from the restaurants and where to sleep without having to pay. . . . I have a thing going now with three good restaurants where I told them I take the food at the end of the day to feed some homeless kids. I feed myself. The kids sounded good, though, and they can't keep the leftover food anyway, so they feel good about it. The Cape is better looking, and the people are richer, but everyone's on the lookout for those lousy teens carrying on, and so it's hard to find a place to stay without being found out. I'll move along here—to Rehobeth and on up—and then work my way down to Florida in October.

There's action down there, and lots of money. They got some trouble with all the immigrants, so they leave old ladies like me alone. I can have a ball until I die—and I guess I don't have too many years left before I get sick with something. I'd rather die along the beach than end up in a charity ward. . . .

Mortuaries and Cemeteries

In a more conservative lifestyle mode, Mary (age 67, Los Angeles, California, 1986) spends a great deal of time in mortuaries and cemeteries, enjoys them, and has wonderful stories about both places. She made a point of telling me that it doesn't matter where a funeral home is in a city; it is the ambience that she likes. Most of the sites in which she attends services are "midtown" or "crosstown" because the cemeteries which she prefers are nearby. Her macabre sense of humor sees her through the services, the often food-laden, social affairs afterwards, and the way in which she chooses to spend her free and nighttime hours.

If I die, at least I'll be in the right place [referring to funeral homes]. I feel sort of good going to all of the services for dead people. They're not me! I can sit and listen to all the speeches and sometimes there's food afterwards. I have tin foil, so I just take what I can save for later. Funeral services aren't like weddings; you don't need an invitation. You just pretend you knew the person. It's better if you know beforehand whether it's a male or female! I once made an awful mistake; it was real embarrassing. But people at these things aren't looking for anyone there who doesn't belong, so if you run out of words, you can just put a hanky over your face and move away. The funeral home staffs just think I'm a kooky old gal who likes going to these things. I'm not the only one who does this, but I think I'm the only one who has to. . . .

Some of the cemeteries are really very pleasant. Trees, flowers, shade when it's hot, and you can just sit on the grass and stay for hours beside a gravestone. I sleep there most days, just sort of curled-up next to a stone, sometimes with a blanket around me. No one dares to bother you. And you can be sure that the same people don't show up very often, so no one complains that there's a loiterer about. And I guess this sounds gruesome to some, but I found a large crypt that I can get into, and it is fine for bad weather. I don't mind the dead; they never bother anybody. It's the live people that scare me. . . .

Nights are bad sometimes. The only really safe places are the cemeteries. But I get bored and then I'll end up riding from one end of town to the other on buses.

Bowling Alleys

Alice (age 59, San Francisco, California) drifted to Los Angeles in 1986 to scout new territory. She had been to all of the bowling alleys and other "pleasure palaces" (her words) in San Francisco, and thought it was time to move to a new city. She noted that the best bowling alleys are where the "average Joe" lives and goes to play and drink beer after work: midtown.

> I just love to watch people playing. I don't have any other place to hang out, so I go from one bowling alley to another, from one skating rink to another, from one golf course to another—you know—like I can spend all day or until late at night there. One of the counter workers in a bowling place got to know me, and she gave me a pair of bowling shoes that were going bad, so I looked like I belonged. I have a sling for my arm, so if anyone looks like they're going to question why I'm not playing, I just slip out my sling and put it on.

> I think people guess after awhile that I haven't got any other place to go, but I think they believe it's because I don't like to stay at home. Maybe a drunken husband, or something like that. In fact, that's one story that I tell if anyone get nosy. At another place, I look real sad and say my kids are all gone and I like to watch other kids having a good time. In another place I tell a story about having bad eyes and can't watch TV like my friends do all day. But the hills of Frisco are getting to me, and I think I'll stay down here this year.

Food Fairs

Food complexes are obvious places for the homeless to frequent. The Farmer's Market in mid-Los Angeles is a very large open-air, patio-style affair where visitors only outnumber the regulars because of the tourist buses. After being a steady patron myself for eight years, I recognize many people who apparently come almost every day to sit and talk and occasionally eat something with their ever-present coffee. Homeless women put their belongings in the green wooden baskets made for the Market, push them up to a table and spend as much time as they wish. I have never seen anyone ask a woman to leave. Martine (age 48, Los Angeles, California) told me (in 1984) how she spends her days and nights:

> I get to the Market about 7:30 in the morning and wait for the gates to open. There are always a few of us, and someone usually brings coffee from one of the first weak batches. Then hopefully some of the bakery stuff is stale and someone sneaks it out to us. We can use the bathrooms, but there is only one free toilet for the ladies. Huh! Men get to urinate for free all the time. Talk about discrimination! Anyway, I pick a table which isn't one of the best so that no one stares at me to move, and I put my stuff around me and sort out what I can use for the day. Like I need a sweater, so I'll untangle snarled yarn that day and then start to knit the next.

> I keep a close watch on who leaves what on a table and just move in and finish it off before the cleaning ladies get to it. There are so many people who come every day—mostly senior citizens with nothing to do—that I don't think I stand out. Oh, I know I don't look real good, but some of the rich ladies put on their old stuff for the Market. Anyway, it's a nice way to spend the day. Lots going on all the time.

> When the place closes, I walk on over to the museum and bed down behind a little garden with a tree hiding me from the street. So far no one has really bothered me. One old crazy man keeps passing and snickering at me, but he goes away. It's nice there at night. I look up at the sky full of stars and dream of living like I used to. I usually have a snack left, and there's plenty of folk who don't go to sleep so easily.

Airports

"Crosstown" often leads to the airport, whereas "downtown" represents train and bus terminals. Sara Anne (age 61, Los Angeles, California, 1985) explains how she lives:

I like the airplane terminal. It's like a self-enclosed city; it has everything, and I can move around a lot from one airline to another, sitting for long periods of time with no one noticing. Some days I just walk all around LAX, and it's great exercise. There is always change on the floor by the telephones and the check-in desks and in the restrooms, and if I don't find enough for food, I just hang around the machines and wait for someone to leave candy or sandwiches when their planes are called. Sometimes I can get pretty good food in the luncheonettes when people hurry off. You got to move fast, though.

I can get showers in the airport, too. I just ask some sweet-looking lady if I can step in when she's through. Most people are pretty nice. I get soap and shampoo samples in stores, and perfume, too. I always look good, and that's the secret of getting away with living like this.

3. Downtown

Some homeless women have discovered how to live in a downtown location despite the many dangers which we associate with that area.

Railroad Yards

Rachel (age 62, Los Angeles, California, 1986) moved from an Atlanta suburb to Washington, D.C., to St. Louis, to Albuquerque, to Los Angeles. In each city she found a safe way to isolate herself amid the downtown throng.

I don't like to be smashed in the crowd. I want to be private. I felt like that ever since I lost my house and was forced to go live on the streets in D.C. I had to find someplace to live where I could find food and everything else but was all by myself. So one day I saw these railroad cars just sitting on a side spur with no one paying no mind to them. I got in by a plain act of God, 'cause the lock on the door was broken and instead of not trying it, I did. I moved in and until, oh, I guess it was about 1978, I made a real home there. . . .

I am always careful to keep the windows covered at night so I can burn candles, and I only cook on my sterno-plate in the middle of the night so no one will smell anything and investigate. Then I'll air the car out before anyone shows up in the morning. Not that many people come by, but there are always a few bums and drunks and kids fooling around. I put up mirrors around the outside so that I can see in all directions from the inside, and I never leave without checking real good. During the day I can open the windows enough to get some air, but I always make sure that it looks deserted . . . .

The best thing was that after I learned how to live in a railroad car, I could go to any big city and do the same thing. There are always abandoned cars in the yards—usually put off on a spur. I just kept moving westward because of the weather. I knew that California had lots of unused railroad yards, and I've been living down here for over a year now. I got scared when I heard that the city was going to take over and put in tents for the homeless, but it fell through. I think I have a couple of years left here, and if I have to I'll go north. Someone told me that I can find a lot of abandoned railroad cars in Canada, and if it weren't for the snow, I'd go now. There are some really peaceful places up there—you know—with no people nosing around and you can just live until you die.

Unused Buses

Abandoned buses are also places for sleeping and keeping one's personal items. Raphaela (age 53, Santa Barbara, California, 1983) found that she could live relatively safely in a downtown location by remaining close to churches.

When I first got here, all the homeless people were sleeping on the beaches and in the parks. Apparently no one wants any privacy. Well, I do. And I just had to scout around for a bit to find how to live without having someone throw up on me. . . .

There are bus companies that store their broken down buses in special areas. They can sit there for weeks, and no one comes around. But I also found that churches often have buses that are rarely used. One church is practically empty of people on Sundays, so I wandered around looking to see if they had unused vehicles. Sure enough, there was a nice newish bus that had dust on it. Someone had probably donated it, but there just weren't enough parishioners left to use it. It's parked way back on a lot near the church, and it's overgrown with weeds back there. I haven't been bothered in months, and I hope to stay here for a long time. I got a sweet deal here, and I don't let anyone follow me. I'll walk around for blocks if it seems like I'm being watched. I do everything but cook in the bus. The smell or smoke might call attention to me.

Libraries

Downtown libraries offer sanctuary during the day. Paula (age 39, Baltimore, Maryland, 1978) spends almost all of her time "researching." When she leaves the library, she heads uptown by bus to a shed in back of a restaurant.

The bigger the library, the better chance of never being bothered. I think I have the equivalent of a college education after two years of steady reading. And I love it. . . .

I go from floor to floor and from subject to subject. If I can get to one of the few sofas, I can be comfortable for most of the day. You're not supposed to eat in there, but I always have crackers and canned juice in my bag. I'll go up to one of the unused aisles to eat my apple.

There are bathrooms where I can wash every day, and the whole place just makes me feel good.

Factories and Office Complexes

Downtown also offers factories and office complexes in which to "hide." Sadie (age 61, Baltimore, Maryland, 1979) lives in a factory and knows women who live in the multi-storied office buildings.

I don't know if I could've managed this without someone on the inside helping me. I mean, he leaves food for me every night. . . and when I come in after six only the night watchman is there—and he doesn't look around real good. I sleep on the couch in an office, and no one's ever seen me in three years. I get a private bathroom at night and there's always good stuff left by the women that I can use. . . .

I know how to get into the drinks machine without money, and there's always change under the machines for the candies and cookies. . . .

I couldn't have survived the winters without the factory. During the day I can stay in the department stores to keep warm, or go to the Lexington Market, or get into a movie. But at night I'm at the mercy of the weather. . . .

There's some cleaning people who let some women into the big office buildings at night. Bless them. Maybe they have mothers who have no place to go and understand. I know they'd be fired if anyone found out, so you won't tell which buildings, will you?

4. Retreats

Religious Orders

An excellent means of securing free room and board is to choose a place which is meant for just such a purpose. Gwen (age 39, formerly from New York, 1975) found a cloistered order in Maine where she could be a marginal member:

These are unusually nice women, even if they are a bit peculiar. They aren't supposed to go outside—for anything. But they need someone to do certain things in the outside world, and one day a special woman saw me lying on a bench in the park and started talking to me. She said that I could come and stay in one of the out buildings and they would provide food and necessities if I would do a lot of their errands. . . .

I had never known about people who live like this, but it is a heaven-made solution for me. I don't have a home or any means of support, and I was thinking about how I'd have to kill myself soon when she came along. I still don't have anything, but I sort of feel proud that I'm doing something for them and I certainly get a place to sleep safely and food from them.

I gave them some ideas about making cakes and selling them at town fairs, and I get to man the table and keep some of the money—which isn't much, of course. Then I barter for other things with the other women manning tables, and I don't feel left out of life entirely now. I wouldn't ever want to go back to a regular life again; this is peaceful and I feel sort of content.

I'd join the order if they'd let me. . . . I know that there's one woman who does belong who is lying about her commitment just to stay, but I won't ever tell on her. She confided to me one day when I found her slipping out a gate to get to a doctor. That's not done; they have a doctor come in. Anyway, she told me how she plotted to get in so she'd have a place to live. More power to her. If I'd thought of it, I'd do it too.

Philosophical Groups

Other retreats are philosophical and yoga centers which allow members to live on the premises. Skye (age 37, Massachusetts, 1976) is just such a member:

I wandered around for so long I never thought I'd make it. One day I sat in a session in a YWCA where a guy was talking about this commune he was setting up, and he wanted to know if anyone was interested. I wasn't until he said that room and board were included. . . .

It's absolutely made for homeless people. I do housework around the place in exchange for my keep, and I don't mind pretending that I believe all the nonsense that the leaders keep talking about! I wouldn't have chosen this location, but it's certainly better than the streets!

I hear there's a new center going up in Vermont, and I'm going to see if I can get in up there. That sounds like heaven . . . .

5. Traveling

Roadies

In contrast to those who wish to "hermetize," some homeless women want to travel—or just have no particular place which appeals as a home base. Martha (age 51, formerly from Memphis, Tennessee, 1984) loves truckers and CB communication. Consequently, she devised a plan whereby she lives in trucks and earns some money by working for long distance truckers.

It all started when I was dumped at a freeway truckstop by my husband and told never to show my face in Memphis again. I was petrified and when a driver saw me crying and bawling that I had no place to go, he let me sleep in the empty truck he was stuck with while waiting for a long distance haul. A couple of nice older truckers sort of adopted me and let me do odd jobs in exchange for sleeping in their trucks. I made money for food by jobbing myself out to other truckers at every stop. Now don't you be getting the wrong idea; I never was asked to do anything immoral. . . .

Well, I traveled all over the country, and I liked the driving better than when we stopped for a change in loads. I had friends for the first time, and I felt needed, even though I guess when I look back on it, they were just doing me favors. I had my own handle—Bootsie, because the only shoes I had were boots that a trucker gave me to wear—and I could talk for hours to all kinds of people. . . .

When I had to have surgery, I couldn't drive for a year, and the guys found me empty trucks to live in. I actually made a home inside, taking lamps and furniture with me when I had to change. I went back to driving with the truckers for a while, but now I stay for a few weeks in one place and then pick up with them on a return trip. I'd like to be married to a trucker, but I guess I'm just not going to find one at my age and in my shape. I'd rather live in an empty truck, though, than be stuffed in some one room cheapie slum place—and that's my only choice.

Conclusion

Whether it be uptown, downtown, crosstown, retreats, tourist town, tracktown, or the beach, homeless women are using innovative methods of surviving in the urban/suburban milieu without ready detection. Living marginally, however, creates situations in which new coping mechanisms must be fashioned. One such tailored tool is to emulate prior lifestyle by remaining in the kind of neighborhood in which ordinary daily life can continue. Another tool is to find a location in which one finds inner peace, such as in a particular retreat. Coping may mean traveling, perhaps from one "busy" place to others. Locating and preparing foods is another hurdle which usually requires new physical and psychological skills. Often the only dysfunctional aspect that a woman cannot deal with is the disruption of a normal social life. While the public may be deceived by a woman traveling in a respectable-looking van or motor home, "self" is never fooled; "self" knows that there is a major difference between the individual who is forced from one stage of life into a less fortunate one and the person who opts for mobility (perhaps as a retiree with a penchant for travel) and has a legal address. While both individuals may be in a transitional phase of life, one has been stripped of prior possessions and psychologically and socially leveled, while the other has simply undergone a metamorphosis of living style without losing status. One is perceived as inferior or unlucky, while the other is embarking on a pleasant adventure. One may be perceived as "crazy" for pursuing inventive activities while the other is considered to be "creative."

Almost all of the homeless women I interviewed engaged in *some* form of creative financial enterprise. Let's listen to these innovative women for clues to (partially) independent living.

Chapter Two

Cliff-hanging Economics

.A wide variety of skills and interests are characterized in the stories that homeless women tell about their backgrounds and current methods of financial gain. There are a few women who live in such places as vans, cars, and abandoned buildings and hold traditional jobs (e.g., office, factory, or store), but more often than not, earned income is exemplified by unconventional and self employment. While personal demons may subtly or even severely hinder performance, if internal voices are not too dysfunctional and external voices do not frighten or otherwise deter participation in the physical environment, one can utilize innate creativity, learned techniques, and inspired purchases to become and remain part of the workforce. Therefore, ingenuity and entrepreneurship combine as the economic form in which an amazing number of lone homeless women can and do indulge.

It is of immense value to be able to blend into the cultural landscape, whether it be in uptown, touristtown, or retreat. Sometimes "creative dressing" is actually an asset; faddish styles often assist and maintain the correct image for a particular environment— Manhattan, Beverly Hills, and Las Vegas being three examples that come immediately to my mind. For instance, layered clothing is in vogue; wealthy women (as well as the middle income group) in many urban areas purchase "separates" which mix-and-match endlessly. Accessories which are knotted, pinned, and/or sashed to the separates are fashionable. Homeless women are usually forced to don attire that they can find (or steal), the pieces of their ensemble—

skirts, shirts, and jackets joined with pins, scarves, and belts—being amusingly similar to outrageously-priced designer clothes. It is only necessary for an outfit to be clean, odor free, and attractively arranged; sizing is a negligible factor in draped styles and color-mingling challenges the imagination. Therefore, a homeless woman in Beverly Hills (or any city in which ladies are style-conscious) may appear to be dressed smartly and consequently be perceived as a natural part of the cultural landscape. It is all the easier, then, to participate in an economic venture in an area in which one "fits." It is not necessary for these marginal women to socialize in the economic environment; all they must do is play a part, in other words, co-exist with others for the sole purpose of making money.

1. Innate Creativity

Yard Sale Yields

Rowena (age 46, Beverly Hills, California 1984) specializes in making "designer originals" from unusual materials.

> You like that scarf, right? [She fingered the one that I had just purchased from her.] Do you know how I got the material? [She didn't wait for my answer. I suspected that she stole it.] You know that yard sale that's pretty permanent on Olympic? Down by the school; you know. [I nodded.] Well, I saw this gorgeous silk that the jerk just threw on the lawn, and I asked what I could do for her to pay for it. She didn't want to have anything to do with me at first, but by the end of the day—and I just hung around—and she hadn't sold it, she said I could clean the whole messy yard up and take the roll. Well, I was in heaven. . . .

> I cut it all up in all different lengths; you know, for square scarves, and long, throw-around-your-neck ones, and thin tie-like ones. And I sat in Robinson's one day and began to sew seams all around the edges—you know, so they wouldn't shred—and a lady was watching me and said wouldn't they look good with pearls and little stones sewn on. So I went looking for all kinds of unusual little bobbles

and jingles in the cans out back of the shops on Rodeo and Canon . . . and then I added some little feathers and gimmicky pins—and look what I done! They're terrific, right? [I heartily agreed with her.]

So I had all these beauties, and I didn't know what to do with them! Here are all these gorgeous ladies walking by me, and I saw them looking at my scarves—you know—I had them all sort of wrapped around my neck and waist and head. They liked them. One woman even asked me where I bought them. That gave me the idea of going to a buyer in Saks and asking if she'd like to buy them from me. I never got that far. Right on Beverly Drive a shop clerk asked if I'd designed them myself. I said yes, and she bought them all. . . and paid good for them, too.

Now I just go from one yard sale to another looking for whatever is beautiful material and then I make things from it. I wear it, call myself Madame, and sell to the small shops. Maybe I'd get more from the department stores. I don't know, and I mean to go in and just haven't done it. But it all made me go in for looking like a fancy lady who's a designer, and I'm getting enough to get by. . . . No one knows—except you and another lady—that I sleep along Santa Monica Boulevard behind the bushes. I just go right into the hotel in the mornings and use their bathroom to get ready for the day. . . .

I been thinking about asking about going into business with one of the nicer ladies who has a small classy shop 'round the corner. If she'd let me stay in her back room, I could use all her utilities and really make a name for myself. Maybe I could end up with my own shop.

Recycling and Handcrafts

Connie (age 44, Wiscasset, Maine, 1976) seeks old tins of any size.

There are lots of throwaway things here. They can be decorated just as if they was, uh, something made from scratch. Like, um, I can make a prettier flower pot or match holder for the long fireplace matches out of a painted and papier-mâchéd can than most could make out of plain old clay. . . .

I dig through all the public trash cans and commercial bins. I clean the cans—it really doesn't matter what size they are—and scrape away as much as I can of identity. Then I build up a shape with papier-mâché, let it dry, and paint whatever suits the shape. No one could ever tell that it is a can unless they look at the inside. I drill holes in the bottom if it's going to be for flowers, or droop the lip if it's for pouring. I make the whole thing a head, or an animal, or a flower, or a shell, or whatever comes into my mind. I can be as creative as I want. Now, for Camden, I make seals because everyone who goes there wants a memento of Andre. In any seaport, I go for boats or seagulls. See, you'd have a hard time telling this was just a used tomato tin.

Using Roadside "Weeds"

Certain urban and suburban areas provide free natural resources that are either saleable "as is" or can be altered easily for sales. Mary (age 58, Baltimore, Maryland) was gathering pampas grass along the main roadway when I stopped to do the same in 1979.

I lived for so long with this stuff that I thought it was weeds. When I was trying to find a relative to stay with in Philadelphia, I saw these for sale in a shop at six bucks apiece. Boy, did I see a money-maker! I just said to my family—who didn't want me there anyway—give me some dough for gas, and I'll be out of here.

I have a real nice little business going. I spend Saturdays through Tuesdays cutting down these feathers. They're just growing wild here, so I don't see why not. Maybe they belong to the state, but no one has told me not to cut them down. Then I go my rounds to some fancy flower shops and sell them from Wednesdays to Sundays. Monday is my day off. I got a book from the library, and I'm learning how to dye the pampas grass. There's more money in the colored ones.

And I can see how I can make arrangements from them and some funny-looking strawlike stalks that grow along the Pennsylvania Turnpike. Now that'll go good around fall and winter holidays.

I found that I was spending too much on gas and car repairs going back and forth to Philly and Baltimore and Annapolis and all, so I decided to make up some cards, get a post office box, and start a business. Now stores contact me and I arrange in advance where I'll be going and how many I'll need. . . .

Maybe I do live in my van, and maybe I'll never be able to afford a nice place to live like I did when I worked for [a manufacturer], but I can eat and buy some necessities. . . and I have my self-respect; I'm a businesswoman.

In the Woods

While Mary takes advantage of the wild flora along the heavily-trafficked state highways, Agatha (age 57, Bath, Maine, 1976) scours wooded areas in and near urban areas for pine cones, twisted tree branches, greenery, and berries.

I didn't think I was going to make it, you know? After all, I got shut out of my house, and I don't qualify for Social Security, and my kids can't support me. Until I got my head together and thought out what was available and what I could do with it, I barely ate. That was how it started, really. I was eating my way through the trees where I slept when I realized how many things were there that I used to make Christmas decorations out of. I just gathered up some of the usual things and began to make what I used to give away: little baskets with berry decorations, table and door wreaths, and magazine racks.

I tried to sell my things to shops, but they make things themselves—everyone's an artist these days, you know—so I staked-out a place on Route 27 and made it look like I was a homeowner who just sold from her house to tourists. Well, I guess someone complained, and the police told me to move on, so I just went on up to Route 1, and that's big enough so that I don't stand out like a sore thumb among all the snooty folk. I don't come down here [Southport] much anymore; I got woods all along the highway, or in a-ways, but there's a real nice patch of dark berry here, and I can't seem to find these near Route 1.

I'm getting better, professional-like, at making unusual baskets—see, mine got these nice twisted vines with the black marks—and every summer I sell more and I raise my prices. I spend the winters sorting, peeling, rubbing, and making the pieces, and then I can spend all summer just selling from morning 'til night.

It's not like I'm ever going to be able to get a house, but I can rent space in a woman's trailer in the winter—like in one corner of her bedroom part where I can put a mattress—and I'm not going to have to eat my way through the woods anymore. Good thing! My teeth fall out!

I found this old car that the dealer lets me pay a little on every month—when I can—and it means I get to have a bed in the summer while I move around. And it's a storage place, too.

Barks and Basketweaving

I found Nancy (age 39, Westwood, California, 1987) collecting assorted flora on the UCLA campus:

This basket—the one I'm carrying my pretties in—I made last year. I sat right in the courtyard of the art building—no, I guess it's really the architecture building, but it's got this nice little place to be artistic—and made my baskets while

the students passed by without thinking anything about it
. . . .

There are so many beautiful trees here that I have a great selection of materials: the cones and needles and berries. And the fallen branches. I peel some. This bark is beautiful. Look at the weather-beaten branches. And the ones wrapped around each other. And here, a perfect spire. This one has, uh, bug pits? Pretty. I went into the library and read up on basket making, and I'm copying some of the masters' works. I especially like the Japanese influence. I wish I could have gone to college and done this professionally—or maybe worked in a museum putting together displays of the baskets of different cultures. . . .

I can sell these anywhere. But if there isn't a student who wants to buy one, there's always the Village, and I've been selling these right on the sidewalk. One woman comes by every week and buys several. I'll bet she takes them to someone who gives her a whole lot more. . . .

It's kind of nice to be able to live and work in the same place . . . Yes, I live around here. In the neighborhood. . . . [She sleeps in the trees edging a parking lot on campus.]

Shells and Berries for Stains and Textures

CoraLee (age 52, Damariscotta, Maine, 1976) caters to artists "because they are there":

There are so many artists on the Maine coast that there's always someone to sell to. That means you've got to think of what they might need. Well, I came up with something unique, or at least I think it is. I'm doing pretty well.

What we've got here is lots of berries and other things to grind up for stain and texture. I've experimented with everything, and I came up with a variety of red and blue stains for using instead of paint—or with it. I grind up some lobster and other shells for texture. And corn, too. I can even stain the shells. That's a lot of time involved. But then

I have to locate the flaky artists who move around, and so I spend a lot of time tracking them and pushing my wares.

The art supply store owners are really interested in what I have, but they want it for cheap and then they make a big profit. I'm not cutting anyone into my pie. Either I make it or I don't, but I've been through enough hell, and I can stick this out because I believe in it. We'll see, won't we? In the meantime, I'm really roughing it. I sleep in any place from my car to bus stations, and I eat when I can afford to.

Anyway, this is better than being shoved around by my husband and giving him any money I make—which is what I had to do when I was working in [a store]. I don't know if anyone would even hire me now; I don't look so good, and I think my brain is sort of scrambled. I can't take too much shit from people anymore; I just lose my temper and leave before I scream. You can't do that in a store. So I'm better off by myself and moving around. I keep on thinking of new stuff to do with the stains. Maybe I'll try some of the mountain towns where a lot of artists live.

Driftwood

In Ogunquit (Maine, 1976) I encountered Lee (age 46), who was selling (mainly) artist's supplies from the back of an old but elegant hearse in what is an area of very expensive homes. I stopped to ask for directions, but I was really just curious about the hearse.

I make paintbrushes and tools and palettes from the driftwood that's always near the water. See, I made these palettes from sanded skinny pieces. Just look at the natural designs. Each one is different. Pretty, right? I sell enough to keep me in food, but I can get along on beer and nuts and whatever a guy buys. . . .

I used to work in a New York fashion house, but when I got fired—the damn fairy who owned the place liked an English queen better than me even though he didn't know a middy from a tutu—I came up here to commune with nature. And look for a guy to support me. I got to commune alright. I finally was down to my last quarter and had to give up my room in a really nice house—if you look real hard from the end of the road you can see it—and I got a job in a mortuary helping with the make-up. Yup. Putting lipstick and rouge on stiffs. I'd been used to it in New York; half the models looked just like the stiffs. Better coloring on some of the stiffs. The place wasn't exactly booming, and when the old guy retired, a son took over, but he wasn't frothing to work, so one of the hearses just sat there getting dusty. I asked if I could use it, and with a little bit of flirting, I got it. . . .

There's plenty of room to sleep in the back, and I got it fixed so I'm reasonably comfy. I made these shelves from driftwood, and that's a nice touch. I just sort of ambled along the highways and byways and experimented with a few things before I came up with stuff that made good art materials. There's lots of artists around here, especially in these fancy houses. They know I'm here, and no one complains that I back the hearse into a side road at night—at least not yet. Some of these old dears like to hear about my New York adventures, and I get asked to tea occasionally. I guess I'm an oddity. Wish I had a real place to live, though. I'm always on the lookout for a decent job, but nothing's popped. . . .

I'm supposed to have had Union backing so I'd get unemployment, but they got together and said I'd quit. What a crock. . . . If I knew who to scream discrimination to, I would. But it's all sewed-up in the unions. Get it? It's a joke. Seriously, if I could do better than this, I would. I got shafted and there just isn't anything I can do about it. So I make the best of it I can, and as long as I stick with the rich, I guess I'll get by. . . .

A Green Thumb and Nine Other Fingers

A van or camper is not only a dwelling, it affords an opportunity for pursuing innovative economics in an uptown/upmarket environment where one can sell street-to-street. Meg (age 49, Pacific Palisades, California, 1986) does not advertise that she lives in her van, but she does advertise that vehicle as "Flower Power." Every week Meg goes to the open-market day in Santa Monica and loads up on small pots, seedlings, and unusual plants. She spends her evenings parked in well-lit lots tending to their growth, and her days selling her wares.

I especially like the ones that make the van smell good even when they're gone. Now take that [a Latin name that I cannot hear correctly on the tape]. After it flowers, which isn't for very long, it leaves a strong scent. At least it does in here; I don't know if it would be that strong in an open room. Can you smell it? It's sort of an orangy odor. . . .

I wish I could afford a real flower shop. I do work a few hours a week in someone else's, but it's not the same, obviously. I have a shamrock thumb. Not just green, but lucky. It's just about the only lucky thing I can claim! I love Wednesdays and the open-air markets. I move around with the rich and the poor and no one knows which I am. Except me. . . . It doesn't cost much to stock up on some of the really unusual plants because they come in in bad shape or so small that no one is interested. But I have the time to baby them, and I can sell them for much more when they are in full bloom and in a cute pot I've made out of some odd thing I've picked up. Sometimes I can use the chipped pots at the shop by making a false border. Sometimes I get the nerve to go down to the flower market, but traffic is bad and I'm afraid of the van stalling. But at five in the morning I can get some good buys. . . .

I know my route. I go from Wilshire to just above Sunset between the beach and Brentwood. But I mainly stick to the Palisades and the real expensive houses. I've learned to talk for a while outside with one or two nice women while I show them what I got, and if I time it just right for certain ladies, they come out to go to the hairdresser or store. Then they wander over to see all my stuff, and I sell to them too. Now I got over fifty customers who I can call on, and while I don't sell to every one all the time, I got a list of what they like and I can ring their bells without having anyone call the cops. . . .

Now no one knows I live in the van, too. I don't know how they'd take that. I got a curtain that I pull across the selling section in the back, and they don't know what I do up front. It's good that the back doors open, so it looks like it's just a truck for deliveries. I make enough—between working in the flower shop and my selling—to rent a cheap room, but where would I find one around here, and what would I need it for even if I could find one? It's a waste of money, and this way I can keep going from market to person without taking anything out. Anyway, I want to save up for a shop, maybe in a coast town down south where it's even warmer. I was thinking of the area just around San Diego. But there's so much competition. I got to find a place with no other plant shops. That means I have to get the van tuned-up and do some traveling. And I'm not ready for that yet. I been trying to get this off my mind. . . See, I had this bad experience a year ago, and I still get scared about being on the road. That's really why I don't go downtown to the flower mart; I'd have to get on the freeway or it would take forever, and I can't bring myself to do that yet. I, well, you're not going to laugh at me, are you? [I assured her that I would not laugh at anything she shared.]

I had an appendicitis attack in the middle of the night, and I got into the emergency room just in time. If I didn't have the operation, I would have died. But I think I did anyway. I can remember lying on the table and getting shots, and then I heard someone yelling, "She's not breathing!" All the pain went away, and I was sort of suspended in the air. You know, like on top of me, not on the table where my body was. I didn't feel anything at all, and I began to sort of float up—you know, towards the ceiling, but there wasn't any ceiling. Then there was a long time when I floated along a darkish alley. No, more like the Holland Tunnel. At the end of it I could see it was all bluish-white. I got to the glowing part, and I was moving along this path toward a really bright light when I heard voices talking to me. I thought I could make out a face or two, like people I'd known in the past, but now I'm not sure. People wanted to know how I felt and whether I was ready to be there. Well, I didn't know where I was! I remember I couldn't seem to get my voice to work, and when I didn't answer, everyone just sort of blurred away. The light dimmed and I began to slide backwards the way I came. The next thing I remember is a nurse telling me I'd be all right, and I hurt all over. I tried to tell the doctor and the nurses that I thought I'd died, but everyone just laughed at me and said I'd been drugged. I don't know about that. I've been scared ever since that it will happen again. I just know I died and came back to life again. So I'm still shaky, but I don't feel as lonely as before, and I started making plans for the shop right after I got out of the hospital.

Within a narrative accounting of her lifestyle, Meg has described an out-of-body and near-death experience—not an atypical example, according to researchers in that field. Her story within a story is not unlike Patricia's (age 57, Roland Park, Maryland, 1979), although Patricia's experience is representative of the traditional phenomenon known as an attack by "the Old Hag," or "hagging" (See Chapter Five for details of "hagging" experiences). Patricia also uses her creativity to "keep on going" by drawing her nightmares:

Sketches for Sale

I saw you looking at my artwork. I didn't mean for these to be seen yet. I just set them out on the grass to plan for the frames. I never really thought anyone would come through that hedge. . . . I know they're strange; you aren't the first to say so. They're, well, kind of personal. I mean. . . they are out of my memories. Out of dreams. . . .

So how did you know I was here? [I told her about a friend who lived across the street. She didn't look happy about being noticed.] I park my van here every night. It's safe. And I can draw without anyone seeing me, being surrounded by trees. Do the neighbors talk about me? [I said I didn't know.] No one has tried to talk to me. Maybe the few people who live on this street think I'm crazy. I'm not. I'm just, oh, angry. At the whole world, I guess. It's been bad times for a couple of years. . . .

I've been selling my sketches to an old chum who owns an artsy-craftsy place. She knows I need the money just to eat. But I've just started looking for real jobs again. It's awful at my age. No one really wants anyone over fifty. And I'm not skilled in anything. It kind of surprised me that I could draw! It just sort of happened. I had a nightmare and woke up and began to draw it. Only. . . it wasn't exactly a nightmare. . . .

See, I'm not just down on my luck. No, I—what happened to me left me, oh, sort of mixed-up. Sid—he was my husband—Sid died and I didn't know that he hadn't been putting in for self-employment, and all I had was a few thousand in insurance money for the rest of my life. I had to get out of our apartment—a really nice one, by the way—and all I could think of was to get someplace to live that was inexpensive and I could be in the middle of things—but in a good neighborhood, of course, like I was used to. I saw the van ads on television, and of all things, that was what I finally did: buy a used van. Some teenager must have had it before me, because it was all outfitted with rug material! I don't like it, but it's great insulation in the winter.

I'd been a volunteer at the hospital for years, and I tried to get a paid job, but they were hiring only young people. So I started to think of what I *could* do by myself. All of my friends had collected antiques, and some of the ladies were like me and needed money. So I went around to all the women in the obituary announcements and—see, here's my card. Discreet antiques sales. I spent a lot of time in the stores and at auctions pricing antiques, and then I'd advise the women what things are worth. I got a fee for putting the woman in touch with the best buyers and then a percentage of the sale.

But something happened a few months ago and it—well—made me sort of—sick. I haven't been able to get it off my mind. All I can do is draw things about it. Kind of. Sid—Sid visited me one night when I was listening to the radio. I mean, I was just lying there staring at the ceiling—the red design on the carpet up there—and the lamplight over there [she pointed to a street light] coming in the little window began to grow and—and well, there was this figure in front of the light, and it came toward me. I didn't move and it came right up to me and sort of floated up over the bed and just—well, jumped on my chest and held me down so I couldn't move. I tried and couldn't. I couldn't even yell. There was this awful smell and I thought, "It's Sid." It was that pipe tobacco smell that I'd lived with for so long. I was hardly able to breathe and I got really scared. Sid was trying to kill me. But why? I mean, we had a big argument right before he died, and I threatened to throw away his heart medication, but I didn't. The smell got so bad and I couldn't breathe, and I knew I was going to die. I must have been on my last breath when I heard the sound of rain on the roof—oh, what an awful tinny sound it is on the van—not at all like it was, a nice sound, on the apartment house roof. We lived on the top floor with such a feeling that it was our house. Where was I? Oh, the rain. The sound startled me and I don't know whether I started to breathe first or Sid disappeared first. I'll tell you, I was sweating and my heart was beating so fast that I thought I was having a heart attack.

I couldn't decide—and I still can't—whether I had a heart attack or Sid really did come back from the dead to do something evil to me. Maybe I didn't take good enough care of him, and he thinks I deserve to die. I should be the angry one; he left me without telling me I wasn't going to be able to live without his income. I don't know, but I haven't been the same since. So I haven't been able to go to the auctions and stores and do my business like I used to. Just a week or so ago I went back to the hospital, and an old friend said I could do some filing and desk work for half a day three times a week, and I'm going to give it a try. Maybe I won't have to rely just on the pictures. I was going to go into pastels and paints. My style is pretty good. But I need a real job.
. . .

It's a shame that there's no place for older women in our society, unless you have money, of course! It's bad enough to get old, but to know that no one has any real use for you—well. . . The only decent thing that I thought of was getting this van and staying in a good neighborhood instead of holing myself up in some ghastly room in a poor hotel. And I couldn't have stayed there for very long. I mean, the little money I had wouldn't have paid for more than a year's rent. Have you noticed that the rents are just as high—or higher—in the slums as they are in the better parts of town? I guess it's all in experience. What you're used to makes sense. It wouldn't make any sense for me—who's used to really good living—to try to make it down by Sparrow's Point, or out in Arbutus. I wouldn't know what to do and it would cost just as much. . . .

Decorated Gloves

Valerie (age 39, Elkins Park, Pennsylvania, 1978) left her abusive husband after she experienced two episodes which are clearly typical of the "hagging" syndrome. She lived in a van while working in a dress shop, but soon began to utilize the vehicle as a base for a business venture:

> God knows why I didn't leave the jerk before I got broken bones. But I was so scared by his nightmarish visits that I was afraid to lie down. [I am deleting all of the material concerning her "haggings."] So I ended up leaving him and all of my things, figuring that God was sending me a strong message. Maybe that's not giving me any credit for brains, but I think I'd still be with him if something scary hadn't brought me to my senses. . . . I got the van and just lived right near the store so I could force myself to go to work and get enough money to get by. . . That lasted about a year and then I only had the one problem: how to survive without working full time—if I could even get someone to hire me. I'm not lazy; I have epilepsy and I get tired real easy. . . .
>
> I finally decided that I could do something in the van while I was resting. You know, like art work or sewing. Something that would sell for enough that I wouldn't have to make 3,000 to make a buck. That's when I thought of the decorated gloves. [She was showing me her handiwork.] I went to thrift shops and got all the old gloves and mittens they had and cleaned them up. The worst part was de-pilling some of them! Anyways, I used dyes and everything I could think of for the particular material. I glued beads and pearls and pieces of old jewelry and orange and lemon seeds as decoration—anything to smarten-up the gloves. Here's some braiding I make from old string I dye, and I make edging from that. Sometimes all around the fingers. See?
>
> Well, I took a bunch to the shop, and the owner loved them, but she wanted them on consignment, and that would take too long, so I went to the first meeting I could find where

rich ladies went. They had a speaker on Russian literature, and was I ever bored. But I put out my gloves on the table beside the programs, and I sold! Every last one of them. I was asked to make more in special colors and patterns, and I've been doing that for a year and a half, and I've really gotten good. Now I'm taking orders from [a department store], and I may just make it alone. I'm grateful for those scary nightmares about Mitch—except that I'm still sure that I wasn't asleep. . . .

Manure and Health Foods

Some homeless women live in an exclusive neighborhood and do business in quite another part of the city. Vilma (age 62, Long Green, Maryland, 1979) lives in the outlying (suburban) area of Baltimore County among race horse breeders.

I used to be a grammar school teacher. When I had to retire because of my health, my husband left me and it didn't take long for me to go through my savings and retirement fund. I would rather die than go to some slum area, so I spent hours trying to think of a way to raise money. I could tutor, but that isn't enough to live on, and I could babysit, again, not a money-maker.

I looked around me. What did I have near me that other people needed? I kept smelling manure from the race horses bred and boarded around here. It took me weeks to remember that people used to use horse manure for fertilizer, and that no one was selling it except out in the country where it happens to be. . . .

I called some in-town florists and asked if they wanted any horse manure. Most of them laughed at me. So I figured that there must be some avid gardeners who moved to the city and were frustrated by weak or dying plants, or wanted to do things the old-fashioned, natural way. I found a stack of paper, spent hours printing out flyers, and spent practically my last dime to get downtown. I put flyers in every residential doorway near downtown Baltimore, I guess. I used a neighbor's phone number, and she was really angry with me in a week's time. There were that many calls. . . .

It's been almost three years now, and while I don't have a big business, it is steady, and I put money on an old van so that I can get back and forth. There's a lot of business in the winter, unfortunately for me, because I have to plod through snow and rain to collect the manure. But it looks like I won't end up in a mission.

Not that I live normally. No; I am almost ashamed to say that I live in a shed on a farm. It's nice of the people to let me stay there, and they even let me pick some of their carrots and tomatoes to eat. I became a vegetarian by necessity, and I actually feel better without meat. I buy brown rice and make a compote of fresh vegetables every day. When there's corn I use that as a base for my dishes. I drink from the same stream as the horses. And sometimes we're there together—can you picture it, the bunch of us bent over together? [She laughed.] Since I am well, it must be unpolluted. I wash there too, but since the water flows downstream to us—and is constantly moving on—it is never stagnant. . . .

I'm looking forward to a bigger business and moving into a real room with a bathroom. I can remember when I lived like a millionaire in comparison, but the strange thing is that I feel healthy. I think part of it is because I eat some of the grasses that grow around here. I eat a lot of wheat grass myself. And while some people put aloe vera on their skin, I get some juice to drink out of it. I mix it with milk and berry juice—crushed and strained strawberries or whatever this peculiar red berry is [she held one up]—and it's good. I know there must be health foods that I can sell also. I keep meaning to get to the library and read up on the different kinds of health foods. But I'm always busy—whether its collecting manure or delivering it, or preparing a meal for myself!

2. Tradition

Stone Sculpting

Dorothy (age 53, Baltimore, Maryland, 1979) told me how she has taken up a craft technique that she learned from her grandmother and aunts.

I'm getting too old for this, I fear. But it's been a life-saver, being able to get to the quarry and find odd pieces of stone and slate to carve or decorate and sell.

Who would have thought that a Broadway chorus dancer—and a good one at that—would end up in the Maryland boonies [actually an exclusive suburban setting near malls, offices, stores, and fast food restaurants] living in a camper and lugging stones from a quarry to make a buck?

Sure is a hell of a way to end an exciting life! But I had no choice, did I? Gamey legs and bad investments, not to mention a couple of loser husbands who left me in the lurch. Oh, well, it's always "buyer beware," and I sure did buy everything myself. I'm resilient. . . I stood and looked at the landscape—that's nice, isn't it? —and figured I might find something I could do to make money. There's that quarry not far, and people buy stone sculpture. I know that. Sculptors run in my family. I learned how to use a chisel and rasp before a fork. I dabbled a bit in it when I was in school, but it was just a temporary hobby. Not now! I looked at that quarry and put two and two together to make three: stone, slate, and me. . . .

I began to carve what I saw and felt from each piece. It isn't an easy or fast process. But I was motivated! This is a cat at his ball, and this piece is obviously just worked to the weird shape. It didn't say anything to me at all. Then this slate here was just a broken square, but I chopped at it until I got a nice shape and then glued down the little pieces of soapstone sculpture. It sort of looks like a football game. That's what I'm going to label it. . . .

I'll put the better ones in a shop on consignment, or hope that one of the owners will buy outright. Last month I sold three pieces and she asked for more. If I can get enough really fine pieces, maybe I'll even get a show in a gallery. But that's just a dream; I know it is. I don't make a good enough impression to go into a gallery and pretend to be an artist who wants a show. But I have a plan for next summer. There's an art festival in town, and I'll have a table with some good pieces on it, and maybe someone will take notice of me. I'll try to fix myself up before then. . . .

Quiltmaking

Marie (age 56, Thomaston, Maine, 1975) makes quilts from scraps of old and unusual materials. She is also (like Dorothy) conscious of not having the appropriate appearance for the kind of business she *could* do.

I don't have much schooling, and I don't expect that I could get any job at all, especially now that I'm past fifty. When Fred just took off, I thought I'd end up at some poor farm, and I had some real rough days for a long time. At a church, ah, [a lot of hand movement while she sought the word she wanted] "therapy" group I learned that I knew how to really do something pretty good. Well, I guess I'm supposed to say that I do it *real* good! I never thought much about all the sewing I'd been doing for years, so when all the pieces of old material were put on the table, I just naturally started making a pattern out of them and sewing them onto each other to make something big and useful. That's what we did at home. . . .

This is from very old silk and velvet. I don't like to brag, but I don't see how anything could be prettier. And it's warm, too. I make these winters, and then summers I put them in craft fairs up and down the main route. I make enough to make the payments on my old motor home, so I guess I'll manage until my fingers go from arthritis. . . . If I could fix myself up to compete with other artists, I'd have the nerve to go to some of the fancy shows. I know what they make for the same kind of quilt. . . .

Animal Skins, Weaving, and Macramé

Penelope (age 39, Damariscotta, Maine, 1975) was wearing her (price-marked) merchandise when I saw her in front of an expensive restaurant.

My cousin has a farm over to New Hampshire, and every year he lets me come for shearing and take away as much fleece as I want. And I also get to stay for the worst part of the winter. I take the shearlings and then have to tease, card, spin, and dye the wool. But the lanolin's great for chapped hands, did you know that? See how nice and soft mine are? [She held out her hand and encouraged me to feel the skin.]

I like to weave and knit, but I really like it when I can get good whole skins. . . . I make them into really interesting— different—jackets. They go over my macramé vests.

My family's been doing it for generations, mostly for fun. Oh, they'd do the church fair bit to raise money for new pews and stuff, but we weren't in it for a business. So it never occurred to me that I'd do this for a living.

So the rest of the year I wander back to Maine and hang around from Ogunquit to Boothbay Harbor—sometimes even to Camden—selling my vests and jackets. This year I had some smaller things like hats, but they didn't sell, so I won't waste my time with them again. I tried to sell through some good stores, but they want your work for nothing, and then you see hundreds of dollars on their price tags. My first year I gave away a season's work. I cried when I saw the mark-up.

I make most of my sales by wearing my things with a big price tag on my back. I sort of advertise myself. It's hot in the summer, and I'm miserable wearing wool when I want to be naked, but it's the only store I got: me. I suppose I look nuts, but unless I put out my stuff on some table at a craft show, I don't have too much choice. . . .

Art and craft festivals are abundant during the summer months, and many communities sponsor indoor shows during the fall and winter. Usually the participation and entrance fees are affordable and a good profit can be made by the artists.

Dollmaking

Susanne (age 42, Albuquerque, New Mexico, 1980) was preparing her dolls for exhibit:

I'm on my way to Tucson for a show, but I've got to make some money for the trip. I'll do okay once I get there. . . . This was really just a fun thing—making the dolls—that turned into a moneymaker. I used to help my mom make figures when I was little. And she said she learned from her mom. It was a family hobby that got started when great-grandma came from Estonia and made everything by hand. She said nothing had value unless you made it yourself. . . .

So I started fooling around with some straw and cloth when I was bored one day. And there was grandma and mom in my mind and I remembered how people raved about those dolls. . . . See, if I twist this main body part just right, I can make this look like the scarecrow from the movie *The Wizard of Oz*. And if I twist it like this. . . and add a piece of wire to make it stay in that position, I've got the basis for a clown. All I have to do is decide what I want for features, and I don't use crayons anymore unless I melt them for thickness and paint over it. . . .

I didn't know what to do after I ran out of money from unemployment, and I really thought I'd have to bunk-in with any guy who'd offer. Thank God I got a part-time night job at a hamburger place and got food and a place to sleep. The manager never suspected that I stayed behind and slept in a little room meant for equipment. I know the morning person saw me at least once, but he never ratted. . . . I made these at night, and I showed some to the kids who came in. They'd ask how I made them, and then a few asked if I could make dolls like a certain character. Well, I began putting a few together with things I found around the place. When the brooms went into the trash, I just took the inside good lengths and began to bind them. Then, you know, I'd add whatever I could, and my first really good doll was the Tin Man. I used all the lids from the fruit tins. One mom asked if she could buy it, and I found I suddenly had five dollars. So I made a few more—getting a little more adventurous with each one—and put them along the wall. Well, all the little girls wanted one. . . It wasn't long before I actually had a line of dolls. . . .

I got a good variety now of movie character dolls, and I take them to all the craft shows in New Mexico and Arizona, and it's enough for now. But I got an idea for TV heroes, and I'm playing with metals for all those goofy alien cartoon heroes . . . . There's a bigger market out there that I haven't hit yet. The only problem is that I have to keep on the move, and that's not easy.

In contrast to those who move constantly, some homeless women cloister themselves in such a manner that they have a place to sleep and eat while they engage in the pursuit of financial gain.

Jewelry-making

Sister David (pseudonym, age 47) lives in a rather unusual church-attached "convent" (not an actual Catholic convent) in Philadelphia. She was buying sterling silver sheet and wire in the downtown jewelry district when we met in 1978:

I make religious jewelry. Not because that's all I want to do, but it's right for me—I mean, it's what I should do. . . I guess I have to call it a barter system, really. I help the sisters make ends meet and they let me stay alive. That's fair! [She laughed.] See, I was on the streets for about a week and knew it was going to get worse than just sleeping at a shelter. I had to get some kind of life going, and I lost my teaching credential—which meant I lost my living. I didn't do anything wrong [she hastened to say] but they sure did make it sound like I did. I had a serious difference of opinion with a principal, and no one was going to side with me in favor of him. So I was ousted without any real chance to defend myself. . . .

One nice lady I knew saw me just hunched over on a bus bench, and she made me her project. She had a cousin who belonged to a quasi-religious order, and she had been kicked out of a rather staid one. Well, she brought me to this kind of nutsy woman in white robes, and instead of suggesting I join her little band, she said I should try to join the better group. Hah hah. If these ladies lead a better life, I surely don't want to belong to the white-robers. The better group works with the poor and haven't got three beans to put together for a salad. The three-bean salad? [She waited for me to appreciate her joke, and I laughed.]. . . .

We sleep in a dormitory-style building and eat communally, and there are religious services twice a day—at which I meditate so as not to be ungrateful. In the afternoons I teach the neighborhood kids who I can interest in doing something more than stealing. Reading and writing, mostly. The group is really broke, and I knew that if I could start a small business for them, they could make some kind of progress instead of always being one foot ahead of the landlord and his heavyweight bouncer. Anyway, I knew how to do silversmithing—I'd learned at home when I was young and did it at the kitchen table—and I made a few crosses and figures—you know, of saints—out of cast wax. Right away the sisters got a table at every church bazaar, and they're pretty regular. We're making money. I've taught them all how to make the jewelry, and if I can find another place to go, I can do that and leave them with a business. I'd really like to get back to teaching, but I'll have to go to another

state and start over again, and I don't know if I can do that
. . . .

Woodworking

While it is common for the rural women to utilize woodworking skills for economic gain, I found that city women also can find good woods and create salable objects. Jill (age 48, Los Angeles, California, 1985) collects odd pieces of lumber from scrap heaps at both private and public lumberyards/landfills.

I look for long, thick strips of wood that have been sawed-off larger pieces. But I also collect any pieces that I can glue or nail together to form walking sticks and canes. Most yards let me go through what they intend to toss. I've shown my finished products to the managers, so they know what I need and where I can find what they aren't going to do anything with.

I've made canes and cane handles from every kind of wood. And I use other materials along with the wood to make both the walking sticks and canes unusual. I use leathers and pieces of bone and metals and anything that fits in. . . .

I sleep in a shed that was once part of a lumberyard. I slip in at night when the yard is closed, and I don't know if anyone knows that part of the fence around the yard moves a little to let me in or not. If anyone knows, no one says anything. I get out early in the morning and take what I want to work on with me to a park. I have a cart to take my things with me, but it doesn't look like the usual stolen shopping cart, so maybe I don't stand out. In the shed I keep all of my canes and sticks, so if I'm found out, I'll lose everything. I am trying to find a locker to store them in, but they are too long. I'll find something, but I usually sell the best ones right away, so if I lose what I have left it won't be so bad. I can always start again. . . anywhere.

My tools are simple. I use about ten knives and files that I found thrown out back of Pep Boys, and I have a small saw and a couple of extra blades. Sandpaper is easy to find in bins behind certain stores and car repair places.

I sell my walking sticks mainly to people who come out of camping goods stores. Hikers all want something to hold onto. Canes get fancier, and when I get a few done, I take them down to Venice Beach and put in with other vendors. They go fast.

3. Inspired Purchasing

Flea Markets

These indoor and outdoor fests have become a livelihood for many women without homes. The Pasadena (California) Rose Bowl is one Sunday venture for several such women, including Lillian (age 52, 1985):

> I've had my spot for about five months now, and I make enough every week to see me through another. I got a good eye for antiques and collectibles, but I don't stock no junk; you can see that. [She waited for me to agree.] I buy and trade with some of the other nuts here, but I spend the week going from one garage and estate sale to another, and I only take the things that I know I can mark up real good. There's no point in hauling something I can only get a dollar on.

> It's fun, and I get to be with people, which is something I wasn't doing after I got kicked out of my apartment and had to live in my car. All my rent money was stolen; I didn't do anything wrong. . . . I still live in a car, but I got a van now so I have room for my stuff. Of course I can't take anything big, and I do miss some really good things because I can't haul it. But this is okay for the time being. When I get enough money together, I'm going in for one of those motor homes, and I'm going to travel up and down the coast to all the big shows. I can see big money there, and I won't have to account for it, either. Not like when I worked for peanuts in a department store and it seemed like I had more taken out of

my paycheck every week than I got. . . . So I'm saving my money and living real close to the bone so I can have a better future.

Agnes (age 63, Old Orchard Beach, Maine, 1975) told me how she lives from one flea market to another:

> I spend the week gathering all the odd bits of belongings that are left on the beach, in restaurants, in hotel and motel bins, along the boardwalk, and in parking lots. Then I add that to my stash from buying and selling over the last couple of years, and off I go on weekends to flea markets. I got my own table, but sometimes I don't even need it. . . .
>
> There are fleas around here, but there are some better ones miles up the coast and a good one in York. If I got the money, I put gas in my old buggy and take a ride for the weekend. I almost live out of my car anyway, so it doesn't matter if I have to sleep on the flea grounds. I know most of the regulars by now, and some of us are pretty queer, but we learned how to get along: by staying the hell away from each other.
>
> I can make a hundred dollars a day. I can come up selling practically nothing. If I can trade up, then I've done good, and I can make money off the trade. I always come back here eventually, because there is so much traffic, and the kids are so high these days that they leave really good things behind. And then there's a lot of businesses here during the season, and that means lots of goodies in the trash.

Collectibles Fairs

The areas near nationally known indoor and outdoor collectibles complexes are perfect locations for squatters to find and sell merchandise. Some people call themselves "pickers" or "gypsy dealers." Sometimes they are simply haulers-for-others who stop to do personal business, and some are outright thieves. Sondra (age 29, Adamstown, Pennsylvania, 1978) lives like a gypsy near several buildings and open-air sales grounds, selling year round to the public and the dealers who know she is there.

I don't smell so good, so you'd better keep your distance. I haven't taken a bath for months, and I don't intend to. But if I have the right items to sell, no one cares how I smell or look. And I do find some rare items left around. Yeah, sometimes I find them before the owners know they're lost, but usually I don't have to take what probably belongs to someone. . . .

This place is a goldmine. I mean, no one can keep track of what they've got. When they come to Shupp's Grove, some of the guys are so drugged out that they can't remember what merchandise they've got. If it happens to show up in my spot, well, I've just got what looks like what they thought they had. I can fix up things to look different. And then you've got Black Angus—filled with snotty dealers— and Renninger's—where there's a mix of snots and regular people—right up the road. On Sundays it's a riot of people setting up and selling and buying, and I just put up my table and go to work. I live with my stuff. I mean right on top of it so that no one does to me what I do to them. . . .

I'll make out. So many people screwed-up my life before this that I'm not going to be kicked around any more. Okay with you?

Antiques Shows

The more sophisticated cousin of the flea market and the collectibles mart is the antiques show which provides ample opportunity for a good living for those who can become "established" and travel a circuit. Terry (age 44, Boston, Massachusetts, 1979) was in a show in Baltimore when we began chatting. She allowed me to tape this (later) interview:

I started the hard way—doing the local lousy flea markets. Somehow I built up a good stock of country smalls and realized that my prices weren't for poor flea markets anymore.

So I had to sell in a different milieu, and the big show at Brimfield—which is a mixture of junk and terrifically high quality merchandise—was my first try at competing with the expensive stuff. I was scared silly. But I sold everything and then bought a few nicer things. I figured I'd better try a real antiques show.

My first year was in small local shows, and I didn't make but my booth rent. Then I went to an estate auction, went absolutely crazy, and bought up a lot of really nice country items which took every dime I had. I got into a panic. What was I going to do with all this really expensive stuff? I couldn't afford a shop; I was broke, and I'd been living with relatives after the divorce, and I didn't want to just turn over my good new stuff to another dealer for the same prices. So I borrowed $300 to enter a good show, and made $2000. It was like bingo: I had to keep on going. . . .

This is my fourth year, and I travel the East Coast all year. I had a junk car which I traded-up for a van, which I just used as a down payment on a used motor home. I don't kid myself. I'm homeless, haven't got much but my merchandise—which is only worth what someone is willing to pay for it—and I owe a bundle each month now on the motor home. I live from show to show. What I do have is a good feeling about myself, and I didn't have that living with relatives and begging for money for food. But I could lose it all next month. This is a real iffy way to live.

For the moment I look good, eat well, and sleep.

Betty (age 58, Los Angeles, California, 1981) not only follows a local antiques show circuit, but is now able to attend shows across the country.

I guess I was lucky because I have an M.F.A. [Master's in Fine Arts] and a Ph.D. in art history. I had—have—a knowledge of periods and prices which gave me an edge in the beginning—when I suddenly realized that I didn't have a home or family anymore and would have to start over from scratch. . . I tried for positions which all went to the younger women—if they went to women at all; most of the jobs I applied for went to men. And they weren't necessarily better for the jobs. . . .

I took all the furniture from my house—antiques—and put out my last dime for a booth at an antiques show. I sold just about everything and signed up for two more shows even though I didn't have anything much at the time. . . . I spent every day for a couple of months hunting for quality pieces that were hidden in basements, attics, thrift stores—you know, all the places that send you into an asthmatic fit. . . Well, I got up quite enough to fill a booth and sell out, and I just kept on going until I found myself enjoying what I started to do just to eat. . . I have a reputation as an expert, and I let people know that I have a degreed background so that when I say what looks to be a throwaway chair is really a cherry half-spindle, I'm believed. . .

Now I'm asked to do particular shows on both coasts, and I can afford to go. The only way I can do that, of course, is to live in my big old truck, and that's kind of fun since it's filled with beautiful antiques! I got that by a real quirk of fate; a dealer went bonkers when he found he'd sold a rare tall clock for pittance—and he just upped and quit the business right there on the floor. He signed over his stock to another clock dealer and then turned to me and handed me the keys to the truck. He smiled and said "Have a good time. I'm going to blow my head off." We all thought he was kidding, but you know, that's almost what he did! He went out and spent a week drinking himself into oblivion and died from a massive coronary. . . or something.

So I just keep on going, and while this isn't what I'd really like to be doing, at my age I guess I'm pretty lucky after all that's happened. . . . What else can an unemployed Ph.D. do except use whatever she's learned in any way she can? I won't starve, but this isn't the life I should have had. And there's no way to save up, or have health insurance. I haven't got any assurance that I'll stay well, and if I do become ill, then it's all over. . . . everything depends on my being able to travel. . . .

Gemstones: Found and Sold

Ginny (age 54, near Newry, Maine, 1976) arrived in Boothbay Harbor with a small sack of uncut tourmalines. She had just finished showing her stock to a jewelry store owner when I heard her mumbling grievance, as did several other people who opted to move away from the swearing woman dressed in every possible shade of red.

Cheap bastard! He knows how much these are worth. Wanted to steal them from me, as if he needed the money and I'm wealthy. My lousy husband treated me better, and he is definitely going to Hell.

I work like a dog to find these. I can dig for months and not come up with anything worthwhile. But when I do hit a vein or a pocket, I really find some beauts. Just look at these . . . .

Now you promised not to tell anyone where I live and where I find these. I'll tell you that there's a well-known mining area not far, but that's all. And then I also know of a place that no one else has found yet. They're digging to put up a lodge or something, and I found these a foot down. [She held up two large pink crystals.] I'm going back now to get into that pit before all the workers find the pocket. All they had done is to use the crane; no man had been down yet. They'll start work again on Monday, so I'm off. Got to get a hitch soon. But I'd hoped to sell these first. I guess I'll have to let this bastard's competition give me whatever I can get. I won't go back in to him, no matter what. I may be dirt poor, but I'm not an animal, and that's the way he treated me. [She did sell the tourmalines to a jeweler three blocks away, and did make a good sale. We shared coffee and blueberry muffins at the wharf coffee shop before she headed northwest again, and she presented me with a small watermelon tourmaline as a memento of our meeting.]

Audrey (age 58, Los Angeles, California, 1986) has an amazing ability to find gemstones in rings, bracelets, and necklaces in the beach areas which adjoin a large urban area, despite a lot of competition from people who scan the sand with metal detectors.

I'm just smarter than most of those beach bums. I look in places that ladies lose or leave things. Like the bathrooms and showers. Women take off expensive or chunky jewelry when they wash their hands or rinse their hair. Then I watch for the rich women who come, and look by their cars when they head for the beach. Every once in a while I'll find what they thought they left in the car. I follow some and wait 'til they leave, and then go through the sand all around where they sat. I found two rings full of grease last week. When women grease themselves up to get a tan, they forget that their rings slip off. . . .

I've found diamonds, emeralds, rubies, and sapphires. I have trouble selling them in rings, because shop owners think they're stolen. So I take out the stones and sell them loose. I make just enough to eat well, buy nice clothes so that I don't look like a transient, and sleep in a motel once a week. The rest of the time I sleep during the day—in movie theaters when the prices are low—and stay awake at night. I save some money in a bank. One of these days I'm going to have an apartment again. It's just a matter of time until I find a *really* expensive ring. Then I'll be okay for maybe a year or two. But I'll always keep doing this. It is better than wasting money on lottery tickets. And I just don't have any desire to work in a store for peanuts. I like doing the unusual and looking forward to every day with interesting people around me. I meet some dillies. . . .

4. Non-union Laborers

The Trucker's Helpmate

In Chapter One, Martha described her life with long distance truckers. She emphasized the enjoyment of the socializing. In more detail, this is her manner of self-employment:

> I built up a real trade, doing special things for truckers at certain stops, like sewing, for instance. Not just the loose buttons and torn seams, but interesting things—like sewing sayings or designs on their jackets, shirts, hats, and pants. I cut hair in a certain style. I clean their cabs, run errands, do their laundry, do the buying of favorite snacks and drinks, do the dialing when they are trying to get through to numbers that are always busy, buy gifts for their girls or wives or kids, buy and write their postcards, clean guns, polish chrome, letter new slogans, set up the schedules, and do all the things that they don't want to be bothered with or never think of. I'm real inventive. I think of things they need. . . .
>
> Every region has guys that specialize in certain kinds of hauling. Like the loggers in the northwest, the hootch smugglers in the south, the hog and cattle pens in the midwest, and the seafood refrigerated trucks in the northeast. Every trucker who falls into a category has different needs. One trip across country I relayed messages on the CB that I was going to be at particular truck stops doing nails in privacy. Now you wouldn't figure that truckers would care about their nails, but women don't want men in their beds ripping them up with dirty and torn finger and toe nails. I did a big business. Then, during one long haul across Texas to Georgia, I had labels for their crates that made it look like they were carrying ladies' undies instead of whiskey. They got a kick out of it. I once lettered cab stickers that said A HOGGER DOES IT IN STYle. . . .

It's all just plain old fun, but I get paid and no one makes me feel like I'm a charity case. And the guys really appreciate being taken away from chores that need to be done and they hate. I guess I'm a homeless businesswoman!

The Itinerant Tunneller

Rae (age 39, Los Angeles, California, 1985) works as an itinerant (urban) laborer alongside men who either make fun of her or express jealousy.

I don't have much trouble with hassling about sex 'cause I'm not anything to look at. Never was. I had to run away from home 'cause I couldn't take being rided about my looks. But I sure do get the jokes and there's some that wish they *could* work as *good* as me. I been known to work with construction crews and the loggers, but mostly I travel with a couple of guys who get steady work in tunnelling. Now I don't like going underground, but it's good money. We go where there's digging and no one asks too many questions. I dress like the guys. I put my hair under a cap, but I keep it short so's it's easier to clean anyway. Most times nobody even notices I'm a girl. . . .

The guys drink up their money, and I did too for a few years. Now I'm getting smarter. Now I want to save some 'cause I won't be able to do this much longer. I got eye and lung troubles from sulfur, I guess. But I'll keep on traveling and working on my own until I drop. I couldn't make it in a regular job. I guess I'm just as weird inside as outside. [Rae is not as unattractive as she insists, but she has angular features and a masculine body type. It is obvious that she tries to look and act like a male.]

The Itinerant Carpenter

Katherine (age 46, Baltimore, Maryland, 1979) works the East Coast as an itinerant (urban) carpenter.

If I stayed in one place I'd probably have tried to get into a union. But I've been a wanderer for so long now that I'm used to traveling from one job to another. I lost any desire to settle down after Ed—he was my husband—let me down, and isn't that why we, you know, women, get involved in a settled lifestyle? Crabgrass and diapers. . . and all the housewifely stuff keeps us sort of bound-in. But not me. Not any more, anyway. . . .

I was always pretty good with my hands. In high school I was told to take sewing and cooking, and all I really wanted to do was join the auto repair class. And woodshop. If it hadn't been for my brother, I probably wouldn't have ever picked up a hammer and nails and actually learned to make something useful. The first thing I did was make new cabinets for our kitchen. A company told my mother it would take thousands of dollars to re-do our old kitchen, and I was so cocky that I said I could do it for under two hundred. I did it for a little over, but then I had to buy some tools back in those days. . . .

I watch for announcements of new housing projects and go to see what's happening. Of course most of the men are union, and then they have their own little cliques. But I got to know some of them over a few years, and when they see me, they know I'm good and they job stuff out to me. When they get paid, they pay me. I'm sure they take the credit for my work. . . . Then I get to feeling like I need to move on, usually because I don't have any place to stay, and I'll hitchhike to the next city and look through the ads. There's always someone who needs carpentry and doesn't want to go through the big companies. I wish I had enough money to set up my own company; that's been a dream for years. But I never will have the money for that. [Her eyes filled with tears.] If I had only known what was going to happen when I got married, then I would have planned something for a different kind of future. Like this.

I guess I've lived for awhile in every big city between Philly and Tallahassee. I head for the South when the snow starts and head for the North around June. I can live in the unfinished buildings—you know, without roofs and walls—most of the places after work; no one figures that anyone's going to be hanging around after working hours. I got my sleeping bag and kit, and wherever I go, it goes. Most of the guys just think I've got too many male hormones, and that's fine with me. No one bothers me. A couple of guys are sure I'm a transvestite, and they've passed it along that I should be watched. I think there's big money on it. Kind of funny in a way. . . .

The Tracktown Saleswoman

Diane (age 54, Los Angeles, California, 1986) follows the track schedules from near San Diego to northern Los Angeles County.

I get about three months in each city, and that gives me time to set up my buttons and bows for each track. I got me one of them badge makers, and it's real easy to draw what I can't take from the magazines left lying around, or from the newspapers, sometimes. . . like I use a famous horse cut-out, or sometimes a smart remark by a tout. . . .

I got some patchwork scarves and hankies. I got some little flags. I got some leftover tickets that were big losers and thrown away. They make fun souvenirs. And then I got my holders for special tickets. See? These hold a bunch so you can't lose them. And then I make these name tags for the tracks so people can sew them to whatever. . . .

You name it, and I'll make it from whatever I find around here before, during, and after a race. I love the ponies, and it's a good way to live without having anything. Not that I wouldn't trade places with you, but I can't fight being poor . . . I had a job for fifteen years and then the company moved and left me high and dry. I was really hit hard. No one wanted to hire a middle-aged woman with a work record of one job and one skill. I didn't know how to do anything that was needed in today's world. The Voc Rehab people tried to find something for me, but no one wanted to hire me. So I just started to fend for myself. . . .

I sleep wherever I can in whatever track area I'm in. Sometimes it has to be in my car, but I have a bad back and I need to lie flat. So I'd rather just lie on boards. I can lock up my stuff in the car and go lie down for a few hours and then it doesn't matter if it's night-time or daytime. There's always a group of track followers to stay near so it's safe enough.

The Gambler's Aide

Lily (age 49, Las Vegas, Nevada, 1984) had been living in the gambling towns of Nevada until she saw new opportunities in spending half the year in Atlantic City.

I've been livin' in the casinos for three years now, and I made enough to get to Atlantic City and back, oh, maybe nine months ago. Ahh, well, it's a bit different, and I think I'm going to take advantage of the new territory. New tricks for the old dog. . . .

There's really better opportunities in Atlantic City, but that weather! Me oh my; that cold just really goes through you. It means stayin' in most of the winter. But the summers are really good there. I mean to live for free and to make some loot. *Real* loot! So I think I'll keep Vegas for the winter and shoot off to Atlantic City in the summers from now on. . . .

I'm so used to steak dinners for three bucks and free entertainment that I'm guessin' that I live better than most homeless people ever dream of doing. . . I can get the three bucks easy on the slots, and twenty-one isn't much of a gamble. But the best part is what I can sell to the dopes who come lookin' for a fast buck and a good time in a weekend. I got my own little business going where I got this list of all the places where you can eat and drink for free and gamble without more than twenty bucks for the weekend, and I sell that for five. I sell maybe, oh, ahh, I guess thirty a week, mostly. I never really added it up, but I get enough to pay for what I need and can't get for free. Ahh, I guess it's more than thirty, 'cause I do okay, really. But I sell other things, too. Like room keys that get left when someone leaves and is too lazy to take it back to the desk. Now that brings in some bucks. They go for a hundred. By the time the hotel realizes the key is gone and changes the lock, I got me a customer who is stayin' in a good room cheap. . . .

I got a lady who'll be a guy's companion, you know, sort of a good luck charm, for three hundred a weekend, and she splits it with me. All she does is tease and get the guy drunk enough to pass out and let him think he's had a good time— you know what I mean—for a couple of days, and then he's gone home thinkin' he's been real bad—and he can tell his pals all about it. But she don't really have to do anything but have a good time eatin' and drinkin'. She's got no place to live either, and we sort of figured we could make more together than separate. . . .

It's funny that I'm livin' better now than I did when I worked in the music store. That was in Kansas City awhile back. God, that was awful. I had to support my husband while he was sick, and we used up all our money on his cancer treatments, and then when he died I was left with nothing but debts. I just walked out on everything; there wasn't no way I could pay back on those hospital bills. . . I tried to get a lawyer to help me do things up right, but I couldn't afford one. I cried a lot about it, but they were going to stick me in jail. . . . I got a ride to Vegas and I've been here ever since. . . .

Many of the stories depicting "creative" financial efforts involve activities which are not totally legal. The women often express dissatisfaction and/or unhappiness with this factor, but I do not hear any actual regrets for pursuing what is necessary for survival. Since almost all of the women have identified themselves as victims at some point in our conversations—whether it be victimization by person, situation, or system—they seem to feel that the illegal activities (e.g., stealing clothing or hotel keys) are defensible in light of the alternatives. When pressed to discuss unlawful behavior, almost all of the women said the same thing: they had tried to combat indigency and resultant homelessness through *legitimate* channels before resorting to current behaviors. Their commentaries on the various types of "politics" which have resulted in lost status and benefits are enlightening. Let's confront the issues.

Chapter Three

Peekaboo Politics

Betty (age 63, Los Angeles, California, 1987) was crying in the driver's seat of her Buick, the door open and a bag of cookies spilling from her lap onto the ground. I had just parked across from her. I asked if there was anything I could do.

> It's like every time I think I'm going to do okay, someone says "Peekaboo! Gotcha!" And there's always something fishy going on. Do I sound paranoid? Well, maybe I am, but I got good reasons for feeling that way. . . everybody's got an angle for themselves, and I mean an angle that's gonna do me no good. . . .
>
> There wasn't anything I could do to stop my husband from takin' off when the business went bad—shoe store, it was—and then all those agency people telling me he'd put the place in my name so's he wouldn't be stuck with the bills. And then those blanking agencies playing games with my bank. And the bank crusts—those guys with the little rimless glasses like in the old movies—holdin' onto my accounts; they had no right to do that, I just know it. But what's a woman to do? So what money I had is gone. . . .
>
> So I finally get a job and start seeing paychecks and maybe holdin' onto my apartment, and the landlord, he sees a way to kick me out and put his kids in instead, and I just know he's not supposed to do that without paying me for relocating. It's supposed to be a law. But the rent control people

won't do anything, and I just saw the same last name listed as one of them. I'll just bet they're related. . . and in cahoots. I've got no place to go at all. And even the cookie company has an angle to flimflam us. . . holes in the seam.

Betty referred to "fishy" goings-on, and other women have pinpointed particular behaviors and circumstances as "collusion," or "corruption," or "nepotism," or "favoritism." The women identify themselves as victims who had no control over situations in which someone used power as a political strategy to enhance one person's status while detrimentally affecting another's. Homeless women are usually articulate about defining *exactly* how their lives have been adversely affected by such "politics."

Victimization is expressed as the dominating reason for a current lack of appropriate dwelling, employment, benefits, family ties, social life, health care, religious affiliation, and ability to voice complaints and obtain satisfaction. "Politics" may involve family associations; secular or religious organization policy, practices, and membership; state and local officials and their appointees; union activities; the medical and legal professions; financial institution transactions; "the media"; private and public sector monitoring commissions; or court system (federal, state, district, and circuit) accessibility and proceedings. There may be one offending act or a concatenation—a chaining—which connects one political strategy with others to create an unbreakable linkage leading to loss of tangibles and intangibles. In this chapter, I will focus on the private sector (although the women note the many connections between the private and public sectors).

1. In the Home

Collusion Among Husband's Friends

Annette (age 58, San Diego, California, 1987) told her story at a shelter:

I guess I was just too dumb to see what was going on. . . I spent my days and nights seeing to it that everything ran smoothly. I thought I was a happily married woman without a care. But I didn't know that Harvey was planning a get-away vacation for himself and a cute child—for the next twenty years. . . . When he told me I could have the house and cars, I didn't know that he had already sold me out. I mean, I was worth about $15. It hurts that everyone seemed to know about him and his, well, peculiarities, except me. No one bothered to warn me that my life was heading straight for the dumper. Not even our best pals— my husband's lawyer and his wife—let on. And then that creep had the nerve to tell me that Harv owed him money and just to be nice he'd take one of my cars as payment! And he did. . . .

I didn't have enough money to hire a lawyer, and the Legal Aid lawyers said they couldn't work for me because it was family stuff. I think they just didn't see any money. And they knew Harv. So one month I'm doing fine and the next I'm left with a house in foreclosure, a car in repo, and my old clothes. [A wave of her hand.] Oh, the furniture. . . everything went on auction to pay months' worth of outstanding bills. . . .

Now you'd think *someone* along the way would have helped an old woman who had good credit and respectability. I think that Harv bribed all of his friends and the people who worked with him. I really do smell rats. . . . I know why his relatives stood by him, I can even understand why his partners—all lawyers—kept quiet. But our neighbors and church friends? Shouldn't someone have told me about his affair with a child, and that his business was petering-out, and that he reneged on our tithe, and that he sold-off all our stocks, and—and. . . *any* of his activities? I mean, he was practically ripe for the front page of the *Enquirer*. . . .

I got nothing now and no way to do anything about it. They tell me I can't even get Social Security and Medicare. . . . and my best friend even said that I have to take some of the blame! Why? Because I wasn't smart. Pooey. People were keeping secrets for him. They ruined my life and now they want me to take responsibility. . . .

Hiding From "Family"

There is more than one metaphorical leash which ties wives to men and marriages that they wish to leave. Syndicate (any kind of organized crime) wives are virtual slaves to their husbands and to the "families" that bind them all together. Connie (age 45, Baltimore, Maryland, 1979) finally had to disappear in the night, go to another city, and change her identity.

I had $553 to my name and a suitcase with what I could cram into it. I waited until Joe was asleep and just crept out of the house, hiked to a main road, and hitched to wherever I was left off. That ended up being Baltimore. I would like to get further away, and this isn't the best city to be in because of the family connections, but I have disguised myself very well. None of my old friends would recognize me, and I know no one I ever knew is going to find me here. And here I'll stay until I can think of a better place. . . .

I don't have a home or any money, but I do have a place to stay and food. He makes me wear uniforms, but that's okay because he buys them and I don't have to ruin the few nice clothes I got. I'm a maid to an old goat of a man who's so mean he'll live forever. As long as he needs someone to be mean to, I have a place to stay. No one else would take this verbal abuse, but to me it's better than what I was going through with all the hoodlums and drug-running. I know I'd be killed if someone found me, but I'm really not afraid of that here. They probably think I went to a big city and undoubtedly they think it's Las Vegas, or New York, or Hollywood. No one would guess that I'd rather be without makeup than without a man. . . .

But this is all from day to day, see? I've got no future to look forward to. I just took the only way out to save my skin. I saw too much and made the mistake of saying I didn't like it. When I asked for a divorce, I made my biggest mistake; Joe had a meeting with some lawyers who scare the pants off me. I think they kill people who don't sign the papers they draw up. In my case, I wasn't going to get no divorce. I might talk. And there's no chance that any other lawyer would take my case for any amount of money; I'm a legal leper.

The Low Self-Esteem Issue

Some women express powerlessness in both losing their husbands and not being able to hire an attorney without buying into the "low self-esteem" theme—even though they tell about their own inadequacies. Sheila (age 62, Baltimore, Maryland, 1979) addresses the reasons why her husband left her for another woman and why she is living in the wilderness area of a dam watershed (at the edge of the city):

> Look at me. I didn't present myself much better when I was 55 and living in a nice house. I can't help the fact that I am heavy, have limp hair which stays white even though I tried to dye it, and have wrinkles that you could plant corn in. I tried to look better, but my husband was always saying how awful I looked in comparison to other women wherever we were. . . .
>
> Now I know that I wasn't at fault for losing my husband to a much younger and prettier woman; the only way I could match her appearance would be cosmetic surgery—all over. I don't have what everyone these days wants to call low self-esteem. I think I'm a pretty terrific person; I simply have inferior looks and that's the truth. My husband obviously didn't love me enough to overcome that. I couldn't make him happy, so he moved on to another woman. He had a lawyer and made arrangements for me to get what he said he could afford, which is $300 a month. He got a divorce and the judge agreed that that was fair. The judge didn't ask me what I needed. Roger got me this old van so I'd have

someplace to sleep and be able to travel. I know what he really wanted: for me to leave town and never be seen.

There isn't much I can do to alter what happened to me. I was a wife for thirty years and ten days. Can you imagine how ridiculous I would look if I had told the judge that Roger *should* love me? Everyone would laugh and I'd die of humiliation just saying it. Who would take me seriously? Can you imagine a lawyer asking for money so I could get plastic surgery so I could get a job and maybe another husband?

Recidivist Marital Con Men

Women often feel that they are not taken seriously, even when the matter is a criminal offense or borders on the criminal. Marital con men are more common than has been explicated, and victims express embarrassment and dismay by the response of the public in general and lawyers in particular. Lois (age 57, Baltimore, Maryland, 1978) was waiting in back of a donut shop for the nightly throwaways when I parked near her. She was disheveled and it was obvious (to me anyway) that she was homeless. I purchased my late-night snack and asked the counter clerk if I could take a bag of the stale-to-be-discarded donuts to a woman outside. She nodded and gathered a few. I silently handed the bag to Lois and slowly sat in my car, leaving the door open. I sighed loudly and munched on a donut. Lois asked if I would buy her a cup of coffee. I bought coffee for both of us, put my purse back into the car and left the door open so that the tape recorder on the front seat would pick up our conversation.

I thought Larry was an okay guy when I met him. He treated me great, taking me out to dinner and all. He even took me to a play, which was a first for me. We saw each other for a few weeks and then he asked me to marry him.

Gosh, I said yes. But too fast. I didn't know anything about him. Not really. He'd been married before, but I didn't find that out until we had been married for a few months. . . .

I was in a market when a woman came up to me and asked if the man in the next aisle was my husband. I said yes, and she said that he had asked her to marry him a few years before. I thought she was lying, but she pulled me over another couple of aisles and told me things about him that no one would know unless they'd been—you know—"with" him.

He had borrowed thousands of dollars from her. Of course he promised to pay back as soon as his commission check came through. They were engaged for a little while and then she got suspicious. She called the office where he said he worked. He never worked for the firm. She told him, and he just made some excuse to leave early that night, and she never saw him again. She said she told the police and they supposedly hunted for him but never found him. She said that her friends laughed at her and lawyers said she was a fool and should have been more careful.

She asked me whether I had given him money. I said we had a joint bank account with a chunk in it. See, my father had died only a year before and left me quite a bit. Larry, he made a point of having my house put in both our names, too. She kept moving us from aisle to aisle, keeping us out of his sight. Then she told me I'd better tell the police, because she was sure he had done this to other women. Maybe someone would pay attention to me, she said. Then she practically ran out of the store. . . .

The police didn't pay any attention to me at all. Some officer just laughed and said it was probably a woman he had left and she was jealous of me. I tried to insist on some kind of investigation, but I was told to go away, that they were busy . . . .

I told Larry that I wanted everything that was mine in my name only, and he got very angry. He refused to change anything, and then he stopped talking to me. We lived like strangers for a few days, and then I went to the bank to get grocery money and found that the account had been closed. I didn't realize that it was an account in which either person could take it all. I was a fool. I knew he wouldn't be home when I got back, and I was right. I went to the police again, and this time they did do a fast check and found that there were other complaints about a man with his description in Virginia. . . .

I tried right away to get legal help, but no lawyer would take the case because I didn't have any money left. A couple outright laughed at me.

Legal Aid couldn't have cared less. I tried the referral service of the Bar Association, but no lawyer ever called me. I asked everyone, but no one saw how easy it would have been to trace Larry and get my money back. He had only worked a two-state area in fifteen years, and other women were ready to testify. . . .

If any of the men I talked to had taken me seriously, I wouldn't have lost all of my money. I had to sell the house fast and didn't get very much. Then I went into a depression. Almost all of the money from the sale of the house went for a stay in a clinic, and now I don't have anything at all. I don't feel well enough to start looking for a job, and I don't know what I'd do.

If a man went into any of the places I did and told the same story, I'll bet he'd have help right away.

Ann (a pseudonym, age 39, Santa Monica, California, 1985) told me the following story during a crisis-hotline call. Later stories characterized subsequent ordeals: she left her husband because he threatened to kill her if she did not become a prostitute for him; she went to a police station and was told that his words alone were insufficient to act on; and while she was trying to locate a free attorney to obtain a divorce and alimony she was sleeping in a telephone booth. Each time she called she was more depressed, and aside from listening to her and advising her of free places to eat, sleep, shower, and talk, there was little I could do. Her last conversation was incoherent, but I was able to determine that she was in the company of men who were drunk and on drugs.

The point I make here is not just that Ann's Jerry is a recidivist, but that there is an obvious cover-up of his abusive activities. Many people and private and/or public agencies could have prevented the experiences which I suspect have led to her death.

> I dated Jerry for a year before we got married, and I knew that he had a pretty bad past. But none of it had to do with being violent to women. . . and he was trying to make good when we married. . . .

> He began to hit me whenever he lost a job. He was okay when he was working. Then he started drinking and taking drugs. I blamed their effects for the beatings which followed. I was wearing sunglasses to hide black eyes, and limping most of the time. My own life was so full of fear that I couldn't think straight. I was ready to commit suicide. I really loved Jerry, and I didn't want to separate. There just had to be a way to reach him, I kept thinking, and I just wasn't coming up with it.

> Then one night we were at a local bar and a girl came up to him and asked about Tina. He pushed her away and made me leave with him. I don't really know why, but I went back there myself and after about a month I saw that girl again. We talked. . . .

> Jerry had had several live-in lovers which I hadn't known about—and 3 wives—all of them molested by him. Broken bones, rapes, strange car accidents where something had been cut, and all kinds of terrible stuff. . . He's a public danger, he is, and no one is doing anything about it. When a woman has the nerve to tell on him to the police, she can forget having any future. Tina did die eventually, and the autopsy simply said it was an overdose. Tina's friends said

she didn't take drugs. Tina's friends also said that Jerry was still seeing her on the sly while he was married. . . .

I've told this before and no one seems to care about doing anything to him. You promised you won't use our real names. I just know I'd end up dead too.

2. In Private Sector Companies

Pension Plans and Firing Practices

Patricia (age 59, Baltimore, Maryland, 1979) was living in a run-down house in suburbs which border on "country" living: homes with varying acreage that were often part of working farms. Changes in ownership and the onslaught of development have produced what can only be described as "mixed" usage and sudden appearances of large, unspoiled tracts of field, stream, and woods. Isolated homes, sometimes hidden from the road, offer the privacy of rural life while being perhaps only a mile or so from streets of house-upon-house. I had wandered up the long driveway to see if the owners were elderly and might wish to part with attic or base-ment contents—hopefully containing the antiques which I needed to maintain a small business and my own economic base. Patricia caught me looking in a window. We sparred a bit about "trespass-ing," one topic led to another, and about an hour later we had estab-lished that both of us were in financial straits. She brought out a tin can with what trendy people call granola and what she said was homemade wine. I did not sample the wine, but the roasted nuts, seeds, raisins, apples, and oats mixture was fresh and delicious (even without sugar). While we chewed, I asked if she would allow me to tape our conversation.

You promise you won't let anyone know I'm here?. . . Then I'll tell you what happened. It still frightens me to think of how I got to be like this. Living like this, I mean—in such an extreme manner—and after twenty-four years and seven months with the company. . . .

Oh, they said I'd get my pension even though they were letting me go right before my twenty-fifth year. But every one
of those rotten men lied; I got a letter from the company
lawyer saying that I was terminated because there was pil-
ferage in my department and since I was the supervisor, I
was to blame. Not retired, mind you, but terminated. I
never took more than note paper and the occasional stamp
from that company, but I more than made up for those kinds
of thefts by working overtime without pay. And no one ever
offered to pay for my cab fare when it was too late to take a
bus and I'd been doing one of those bastards a favor by
finishing work he'd get the credit for. That lawyer lied to
protect the company executives. There wasn't any way I
could prove it, though. . . .

I had only a few thousand dollars saved up in the bank, and
I finally did go to a lawyer. He wanted a $5000 retainer
before he'd agree to take the case. I was caught between
clearing my name to get my pension and poverty, so I gave
him the money. Then I had about $2500 left to live on, and
with the rent, winter utilities, and food, I only could keep
my apartment for a few months. . . .

One of our clients owned this farm, and I had had occasion
to come out here to have the Mr. sign papers. He died
before I was fired, and the Mrs. was here all alone, and I was
the only one from the firm who even called her to see if she
needed anything. She died just before I left. She was child-
less and I knew from their file that there were no heirs. So I
reasoned that the farm would go up for sale by the bank.
Which it would have except for the problems with the ef-
fluent from the stream on the property. Someone had to
take charge and really find the source of the problem, but no
one did. The house just sat here with no one particularly interested in it, and no really close neighbors to care. . . .

When the panic became an everyday feeling, I began to
think more clearly about where I could go, and I kept think-

ing of this place. Sooner or later someone from the bank will assign this property for sale, but from their past hesitance, I think I may just be here for a long time. I hope so, because I don't have any other place to go. I can plant a few things for food because there's still some good soil left on the east side, and there's a cow who I hide way out in back of the property, and she's fine for milk, sour cream, ice cream, and yogurt. I keep just a few hens and a rooster, so I have eggs and the rare chicken dinner. . . .

After maybe half a year the lawyer decided he didn't want to continue, but of course he kept the retainer. I went to Legal Aid, but the man just looked at me as if I were mad. "We don't take cases like that," he said, and I knew that I was sunk forever. I'll bet I have a legit case, though, and even though I sent off letters asking for a lawyer from the Bar Association's Lawyer Referral Service, no one offered to take the case. I know these men all know each other, so they cover up a lot. I'm a nobody, so no one is going to pay attention to me.

I kept in close touch with Pat for about a year—until I left for California. While I never assisted her with any sales of the antique furnishings in the house, I am quite sure that she began to sell household valuables in order to raise money, probably to dealers with whom she could remain anonymous. Certainly she would not invite anyone out to the house, so she must have taken selected items to shops or shows. (There was a car in the garage.)

Sexism and Ageism

Women have been forced from organizational settings by men who plan to replace them with younger—and often prettier—females. Susan (age 57, York, Pennsylvania, 1979) says she was not surprised at the event and had tried to find other employment in anticipation of being a less desirable, older working woman.

I've worked since I was twenty. I've really been a workaholic, trying to get as high as I could in my field. My whole life has been sublimated to getting ahead, because I knew that I wasn't popular with men and the chances of my getting married were slim. So when I finally became secure in my job, I was very happy.

When my forty-first birthday sneaked up on me and I was subjected to some jokes about it at work, I began to think about my security. I looked around me and didn't see any older women. I kept seeing those I knew from my generation disappear and young, long-legged blondes showing up at their desks. I started looking through the newspapers for executive secretary jobs. I mean impressive ones like the one I had. I went on a few interviews out of town just to see what would happen. I never got a nibble, and I am very qualified. I checked to see who got the jobs, and in every case they were young, attractive women. . . .

On my forty-sixth birthday my boss said he was considering the necessity for his secretary to accompany him on business trips. I said that was fine with me because all I had was a cat. He struggled to make excuses why I just wouldn't be an acceptable assistant. I got the message and earnestly tried to find another job. I had interviews galore, but not one offer. A year later I got formal notice that I was being transferred to another man and department. I didn't know anything about accounting and I knew that I would not be able to make the transfer properly. I protested to the chief executive of the corporation, but he said my boss could hire and fire anyone he worked over. That old man had a twenty-two year old secretary who typed with one finger. I was let go, of course. I'll bet those two old goats had a good laugh at me.

I had a bank account. I had a nice apartment. I had nice clothes. I lived quietly and pleasantly for a few years without a job, but I never stopped looking for something suitable. All I have ever been offered is a temporary secretarial position, and the pay is low. Last year my money ran out and I thought of suicide. I can't imagine living and eating in missions. I certainly can't get by with the small check I get every month; it is just enough to buy food and personal necessities with. It won't pay for an apartment or even a decent room anywhere.

I'm homeless right now and am not on the sidewalk just because I've been living with a friend. But she is going to live in New Mexico with her daughter. I don't know where I'll go from here. Oh, by the way, I was replaced with the prettiest redhead I've ever seen. She got a divorce right after she was hired, and she's been traveling ever since. It seems to me that all of us who aren't bosses and over forty are on the way out. It's just office policy, and unless you have some power or influence, women can expect to be given the nudge after forty-five and certainly after fifty-five. When we've given our lives to the company, how do the bosses think we can live after fifty? There should be assurance for us.

Mergers and Liminal Positions

Some homeless women tell stories about being passed-over for promotion in organizational settings, often becoming liminal members who are essentially positionless until formal notice of termination. Rita (age 47, Los Angeles, California, 1985) was introduced to me because she was a battered wife who had left her home. It was not until we were talking about her opportunities for employment that she revealed her previous experience as an executive with a financial institution.

I made over $50,000 a year and had a Mercedes. When a merger was in the works I knew that I was going to be in a different position than the male executives. They were being courted by both sides while no one really paid much attention to me, despite my superior ability. There just weren't any women in top positions in the other company. . . .

The day came when we celebrated the merger, and I didn't really know where I was going to fit in. I was due for a promotion with a big raise in the next fiscal quarter—the highest position in my particular area of expertise. Some celebration. The men were all bombed on champagne and I was wondering if I still was on the payroll. No one had said anything.

I worked at my same old desk for a few months, and then the time came for promotion. I arrived at work one morning to find a sealed envelope on my desk. I was not fitting-in with the proposed image of the new corporation, and a young man was going to be taking over my accounts. I blew my stack, but it didn't matter. I wasn't on the insiders' network and I was expendable. I got severance pay but no recommendation, and that kept me from getting other employment. I hired an attorney to file a suit for discrimination, but somehow he didn't really put his heart into my case. I knew that when I saw him having dinner with his wife and the corporation boss and his wife. They were all just a little too cozy, and when my lawyer said the company president noted that I was not good with personal relationships, I knew I had lost my case. I was very popular. . . .

It was when I started staying home that I realized that I had been hiding my domestic problems with work. I would just go to the office and really forget about life at home. Now I don't have a home or a husband or a job. I went through my savings and now it's just what I can pick up on small private jobs.

Relocation Policy

Companies use "relocation" as a way to remove people from jobs which they would not otherwise leave. Susie (age 50, Baltimore, Maryland, 1979) blames company policy for her current homelessness:

I guess I went too far too fast. I took the jobs which I know men wanted—men who had been hiding in the company corners waiting for some job to come up that they might be able to perform. It was just too much for them to accept that a woman might be better in a traditional male occupation, and I was the only female exec.

I heard rumors that there were complaints every time I was promoted. I didn't think I was making real enemies, but I suppose the big brass upstairs were annoyed every time one of their relatives nagged for a better place in the company and there I was in it. . . .

There were always some small acquisitions and every time a new plant opened, some top men were asked if they wanted to move. They had the opportunity to refuse. I wasn't asked to go to any of the other locations, but when one came up in northern Arkansas I was the first one to be named. I didn't want to go there. I said so. I was told that if I didn't go I would be fired for noncompliance. I got a lawyer and he said I didn't have a prayer. I took a leave of absence to see if I could find something else of equal importance, and while I was gone my job was just eliminated. My lawyer said I had no case: the company had the right to make the policy.

I haven't found any other employment yet, and I guess I have to admit I may not do so.

It's just a matter of time before I also have to admit that there's not ever going to be any money coming in. Then I will be up the creek and plainly classified as just another poor woman. And all because I was better than most of the men in the office.

Favoritism and Union Problems

Same-sex preference situations affect some workers via intra and inter-office politics. Sondra (age 44, Richmond, Virginia, 1979) believes that she was the victim of such personalized discrimination:

I had a pretty good job for twelve years and eight months. No complaints except the usual: short lunch hour and instant coffee breaks with phone calls interrupting. Then I started noticing that my boss—the head of purchasing for the store—was acting funny. She was all bright and breezy and dressing up when her normal behavior was glum and her favorite color gray.

All of a sudden my work wasn't good enough. All kinds of odd notes came my way about what I should have done or how I wasn't showing promise. I showed the notes to a guy who did the window dressing, and he just smirked and said I certainly was innocent. . . I never really understood at all until the day this new woman showed up and started following me around. She acted like she was my shadow, making notes and running off to have little chats with my boss. Boy, was I dumb. I even told her my hints for success.

If I had known that the boss was looking for a lover, I might have had the nerve to at least seem interested in being with her. Not that I could fool her, but maybe she was just lonely. I don't know, but one day I got the pink slip and the next day the hoverer was in my job. When I took the problem to the union, I got this brush off. You know, "What makes you think you got bounced for anyone in particular? Maybe you just weren't up to the job." That was a double smack in the face; first my boss and then the union liaison. The window dresser said that there were lots of gays and lesbians in the store and anyone who wasn't just wasn't in the club. Well, I knew that he was, and I never cared. But when it cost me my job and put me on the street, then I want some action. . . .

I wrote to the company president, figuring that maybe he'd care, and I got a letter from his lawyer saying that I'd better be careful about spreading rumors about the department head's lesbianism. What a closed system it was! It was like having family pull. . . .

So I came up here [Baltimore] to look for work, but without a referral I don't stand a chance of getting hired. I have to say where I've been working for the last twelve years, and they'll check. I'm sure to be called something bad. I don't have the nerve to tell the truth; with my luck my interviewer will be a lesbian.

Non-tenured Teaching

All teachers (and grammar and high school teaching assistants) know the hazards of their profession. Advancement and security at the college level usually means publishing and peer recognition. Ann (age 44, San Francisco, California, 1987) was an assistant professor who did not obtain tenure:

> I worked so darn hard, teaching more classes than some of my cohorts, and publishing more articles than a lot. And I had two books which were bound to be published soon by a university press. . . I felt safe. There weren't many full professors in my department, but none were women. I really didn't think I'd have a problem, though, because I was always in demand for conference chair or discussant. I expected to obtain tenure. And then this little twerp began a campaign to get the opening created by a retirement. . . .
>
> Well, it was amusing, and we all laughed at his machinations. He was so obviously ill-equipped to fill the spot. But he sure was thorough in shoe-kissing. He suddenly was the choice for taking over the retiree's teaching area even though he had never taught those classes before. . . .
>
> I didn't get tenure and had to look elsewhere. It's difficult for a woman to locate a university position anyway, but I had this twerp sort of dogging my tail with stories of how I wasn't up to par. I know his networking lost me at least two positions I could have handled with ease. Anyway, I was reduced to working in an office for a living, and after two years I was heading for a nervous breakdown. I even thought about suicide. . . .
>
> I'm not doing anything right now, and I'm just living from day to day. I know I won't be hired by any college now, and I hate working in an office. I would rather be dead than have to look forward to that all day for years to come. So I

send out resumés and show up at conferences now and then, hoping that someone will offer a teaching position. Totally futile. The twerp has married a young comer with my specialty area, and he's looking for a position for her. I have no references other than my old department cronies, and they won't write any recommendations for me now. My day has past. . . .

3. In Fraternal Organizations

Sorority Shenanigans

Carole (age 53, Los Angeles, California, 1986) was a sorority housemother for many years:

I thought I'd be able to end my days there, probably with a little pension from the national Board. Little did I know that just when I would feel secure, an ex-sorority member would want my job. I didn't have much notice, and I found out that I wasn't going to get any real severance pay, either. . . .

I had taken the job when I got kicked out of my home after my father remarried and his new wife didn't want me around anymore. I didn't have any education which provided me with more than how to teach the violin, and being plain, I knew I wouldn't marry. So being a housemother seemed like a good place to have a home and a family. . . .

What bothers me is that I was doing an exceptional job, and all it took was an ex-member of the sorority saying she needed a job—and I was just deleted like an unwanted page in a book. It's as if I never was a real person there, just a filler. I made that place into a home for the girls and I thought that it was appreciated by national. Apparently all they care about is keeping their past members happy.

Private-Public Cronyism

A private organization may be associated with public office power in the outcome of a woman's future. Shirley (age 48, Portland, Maine, 1975) told me how her husband's fraternal organizational connections played a part in her loss of home and support.

Alan was an active member of his local chapter, and his best buddies were the town officials. That included the police and judges. Whenever any cronies were in trouble, they just laughed and said that Tom or Jim would get them off. That went on for years, and naturally it was just a joke to me. Until I discovered that it went way too far. . . .

I had wanted a divorce for a long time because my husband didn't just have a wandering eye; his hands and genitals were always in someone else's pants. It was embarrassing because everyone knew about it. You can't hide adultery in close communities. I knew that other women were talking behind my back, and I finally just threw up my hands and filed for a divorce.

I didn't count on the fact that there was hardly a lawyer or judge in our district who didn't belong to one of these private organizations which males like to join. You know, with the funny hats, and secret handshakes, and all that baloney about being blood brothers. I wouldn't be at all surprised if my own lawyer didn't put my husband's interests first, but his lawyer and the judge certainly did. My husband had the nerve—no, the gall—to say *I* was the adulterer—or is it adulter*ess*? There wasn't a soul in a fifty mile area who didn't know about my husband's infidelity, but the judge—who lived right in the middle of the district—made the decision that my husband had the right to a divorce and everything that went with it.

I was appalled, but there wasn't anything I could do about it. I couldn't *prove* they had had meetings and decided how the case would end. I was dumped out of my house, provided with a car that had 120,000 miles on it, and told to take off. I was so mad that on my way out of Portland I walked right into a lodge meeting and threw a spoiled egg on the president's gavel. I yelled at the men, accusing them of being as rotten as the egg. Then I ran. I drove nearly a hundred miles before my blood pressure came anywhere close to normal. . . .

I went to my brother's house, but I could only stay there a little while because he has a large family and no space. I've been just roaming for a year now, and I've been thinking that maybe I could join some organization which has a place for its members to live.

4. In Religious Organizations

Personal Gratification and the Neighborhood Church/Temple

Sometimes we do not consider that there is a "political" aspect to ordinary religious affiliation. The ways in which we are treated in local religious institutions have strategic implications—both social and in opportunity to participate in community "good deeds." Sharon (age 65, Philadelphia, Pennsylvania, 1979) expresses what many women recall as "some of the best times I ever had":

You know, I belonged to both a church and a temple; that's right, you heard me right. I was a devout Presbyterian before I married, and then I joined the temple my husband belonged to. I mean, well, I converted first so he would be happy, but I really kept on going to my own church. He never cared. . . .

Every Friday night we went to services at the temple, and there was always this great feasting thing going on, and terrific chatter and lots of invitations went out for the next week, like bridge and canasta and dinner. . . and every Sunday I went to church and afterwards my friends and I went to brunch and talked about the new wing and the children's program and all the gossip. . . and at both we spent some time in talking about charities and the time we would spend in helping others. . . .

When I lost Joe suddenly, there was this quick response and I was kept busy by all my friends. After about maybe, oh, three months, I was sort of forgotten, and less and less was I included in things. It really didn't have to do with Joe being *along*, you know? He didn't go to the weekly things with me, or the Sundays neither. But—well—maybe I'm imagining things, but I think I was more important being married and having money to go and do with. I got poorer and poorer and when I had to give up my home, I couldn't have lunches at my place. I was in one room after awhile, and my clothes were getting shabbier, and I was ashamed to go to any of the really nice affairs. Even on Sundays, when I was used to being part of the altar decoration committee, even then I didn't want to get up in front. . . .

All of the members sort of forgot me when it came to anything at all, and I just dropped out of both places. . . . I cried so much over losing those people. I never thought much before about having a good time putting in my hours at the hospital or stuffing envelopes when we were raising money for our orphanage, but those were some of the best times I had over all the years. It hurts when I think that it wasn't just me people wanted around, but what I could do for people I thought were real friends. . . .

Using the Church for Regeneration

Jane (age 53, Eastern city, 1978), a lifelong Catholic, decided that her church was going to save her from homelessness. She created a shadowy entrance into the very "politics" of church life and hierarchy to fulfill her plan for a future.

I had been homeless for about seven months and I just would not go to one more mission. I had had a lovely home and good food on the table for too many years not to plan for something better than being a drifter with absolutely no future. So I spent weeks on developing a plan to make sure I'd, you know, succeed—be accepted.

First, I went to the Catholic Church in [a major city] and told a priest that I had been having visitations from St. Anne. I even said it as part of a story in the confessional, so that if the priests got together, they'd agree that I'd been seeing St. Anne. I said I was afraid of the visits because she was telling me that I was to become a nun in a particular order. I was supposed to spend my life helping old and ill women. . . .

I must have been a really good actress, 'cuz a priest did some calling around and for the time I was in [the city] I was put up in a church building—an old rectory, I think. About three weeks later I was brought down to [a city] in a big black car and introduced to the sisters here. I was questioned a lot, and we talked a lot about Catholicism, and well, I don't know all that went on, but I stayed and after about two years I was allowed to take my first vows. . . .

I've been a nun for three years, and I'm not ashamed of what I did. I really do work very hard with needy women, and I don't think God will punish me for being inventive. I haven't hurt anyone, and in fact I've saved several women from committing suicide. . . .

You promised not to reveal my name, but you know that if you break your promise, I'll just call you a liar and I will be the one believed. I'll do almost anything not to be put out onto the street again.

In Community Organizations

Frances (age 59, Santa Monica, California, 1987) represents many now homeless women who were once extremely active in local and grassroots activities. By far the most prevalent references have been directed to specific women's organizations, their choice of issues, and the manner in which in-fighting took attention away from the

mainstream woman and placed emphasis on special-interest matters. Frances and others place at least some of the blame for their
present status on related organizational friction.

It was a time when women were just getting into local activism, and I chose to volunteer for NOW. I was there when
all the planning was done, the placards were cut and the
slogans decided on and hand-printed, and the parties and
fundraisers were held. . . And I spent a lot of money helping
with the office needs, and a lot of time helping with taking
other women's volunteer time. . . I was always ready to step
in and do more than my share. . . .

Of course there were personality problems, but we had a
greater purpose. . . and so I let other women argue about
times and places and who was going to do what. . . and let
everyone walk all over me. But I didn't mind it then; I really
didn't. I had my place in the scheme of things, and I have a
good nature. But things got rough when things started to
fractionalize; is that a word? Or is it factionalize? Oh, well,
you know what I mean, don't you? Two groups of different-
thinking women get started and begin to fight, oh, you
know, spar, over who is tops and who gets credit, and what
issues are going to be put at the top of all efforts. That was
the worst part. I wasn't even interested in what finally became the hot issue, and yet I was expected to act like I was. I
didn't even want to get involved in what I think are. . . personal women's problems. . . and there I was, in the middle
because I didn't want to take sides.

I didn't like at all the women who were taking over. We had
absolutely nothing in common, and they were making [the
issue] the only thing that was supposed to be worthwhile in
NOW. I was asked to march for [the issue], and I didn't really want to be seen with those women. I didn't want
everyone to think I was one of them. I was forced out eventually because I wouldn't take their side and become visible
as pushing [the issue]. It made me so upset that I took it out

on my husband, and I know it was my fault that he took up with a much nicer person. I got to be an awful bore on NOW problems, and when he asked for a divorce, I couldn't even muster up an argument. . . I didn't even ask for much and I didn't get what I need to live. It's my fault, but the result is the same: I'm without funds and a place to stay. I don't even have any friends to turn to because I gave all my time to NOW.

When I asked for some assistance, oh, mostly referrals—for a job, and a room in exchange for housework—no one there even talked to me in a nice way. You'd have thought that I was a stranger instead of donating about ten years of my life to those women. . . .

The women's movement is a big joke. If you've got the interest in pushing whatever the leaders want for their own personal reasons, then you've got a spot. But when the issue changes, and the leaders change, you'd better be ready to close down your own feelings and just be a sheep. I've seen it happen in all the special women's groups. You get factions and they fight and only the insiders get to do the planning. And the issues get so narrow that it isn't helpful to most women. . . .

In Commune Life

Most women who scheme to join religious or philosophical organizations simply to attain food and lodging understand the politics involved in gaining and keeping the good graces of the leaders. Most women are also careful to choose groups which are "legitimate." Two women with whom I spoke were desperate and joined what can only be described as a radical sect. I did not have the opportunity to accurately document the stories of the ladies who joined Reverend Moon's "Moonies" (with a base in Towson, Maryland in the 1970s) or of two women who travel from one yoga center to another around the country, but I did talk at length with a woman who joined the Oregon group led by the Bhagwan Shree Rajneesh. Hillary (age 44, originally from Chicago, Illinois, 1986) left the commune when she inherited an unexpected amount of money and a home in Los Angeles. I was in an audience when she was talking about her past experiences at the commune, and went to chat with her after the program.

I told a little bit about why I joined, but the real truth is that I was homeless and saw a chance to be part of a budding community. I didn't care if they were all a bit nuts; I suppose I was too, after what I'd gone through.

I had tried every which way to find a job and start a new life after a divorce in which I got nothing. But after I had been homeless for four months, I didn't look good enough to go for an interview. Then I heard these people talking about living in a healthy valley with clean places to live and good food and new friends. Well, it seemed to be tailor-made for me. I walked right up to one of the smarter-looking women and said I believed it was a great idea.

I had my way paid, and I was really impressed in the beginning. Then I learned that I was expected to have sex with any man who wanted me, and I figured out how to be especially unattractive. That didn't fly well, but it did get me off the hook. . . I got to stay celibate.

No fun, but safe. I didn't mind that most of them were fanatics and some outright mentally ill. We all worked together, and I had some nice lady friends. The food was good. The place was clean. I had a home again, even if it wasn't my ideal. I was working my way up the power structure by offering advice on how to get more labor out of the young men, and I liked being in charge of a unit. I had some say-so over life.

When I had been there for, oh, maybe a year and a half, one man wouldn't take my "no" and I was brought up before a, well, like a tribunal, and told that I had to follow the rules or be expelled from the commune. I was wondering what to do when I got a letter by mistake; we usually had our mail censored before we got it. I had an aunt that I'd only met a few times, but she died without other relatives and I inherited her estate. I got into town fast and made a collect phone call to the lawyers. They paid for my bus fare down to L.A. . . .

I would probably be hunting for another commune if this hadn't happened. I refuse to live like the other homeless women, on the street or in missions. They have no say-so over their lives, and I decided that whatever little power I have over my life is going to be used to the fullest. Unfortunately, the communes take away most of your self-determination, but I learned how to stay in the background sexually and use my strengths in economics. But it didn't matter in the end. There was much stronger power than I could maneuver around. I've never seen such organized chaos.

In the Media

Also in the shadows of organizational politics are women who have been "relieved" of media jobs. Jacki King of Los Angeles was quite vocal during 1987-88 about her experiences as an anchorwoman who was fired and has become homeless as a result of an inability to obtain any subsequent employment in her field. I have not interviewed her, but she is occasionally invited to speak about homelessness (and her personal experiences) on television "talk" shows. The last time I saw her (in mid-1988), she was telling a story with a new theme—of being the object of dual victimization by an individual with whom she had had a personal relationship and the media politicians with whom this man networked.

The subject of dual victimization is a very common one among homeless women. Usually the woman has been the victim of an individual (e.g., a violent husband), and then been ignored or the recipient of inadequate assistance by "the system."

5. In the Private Agency "System"

Counseling Failures

Corrine (age 53, Baltimore, Maryland, 1979) explained how she became homeless:

> After I left one abusive husband, I found that I had chosen a worse example of a spouse. He was a drunkard who beat up on everyone. So when I went to counselors that were recommended by just about every place I called, I was told that he had to help himself and I had to stop being an enabler. That meant that I had to find a way to make money for myself and let him starve. Well, I got a nothing job and tried to get along, but I did so well that I got advanced and got good money. When my husband saw that, he really quit his job for good and then filed for a divorce and alimony....
>
> I could just kill all those wonderful counselors. They really screwed-up my life. Now I have to work hard to support that bastard. You know why? Because when I went to court I had the attorney and the drunk asked for sympathy since he was so ill that he couldn't afford one. The judge agreed: alcoholics are ill and should be afforded every opportunity to be assisted by the system. Well hell, why wasn't I assisted by the system? I was the one who had the broken arm and the concussion and the scars. The fact that he was excused because he was ill is disgusting. I ended up being a victim of him and the most stupid system I can think of. Now he gets free counseling for his drinking and he isn't dumb enough to ever admit that he can stop—or has stopped. That means that I have a choice of quitting my job to stop his alimony—and starving myself—or staying in a job, eating, and support the bum forever. What a lousy system! It's like everyone is in cahoots with everyone else in power and the focus is anywhere but on the victim.

Have I shown them? Of course I haven't. I did quit my job because I got ulcers from all the disgust I felt. It was starve or die of a bleeding ulcer. What a choice. But I wasn't going to spend the rest of my life supporting that bum. So now I lost my apartment and live on welfare. I'm sleeping in libraries and malls during the day and walking the streets at night, hoping I won't be attacked. . . .

The system stinks. There certainly isn't any assistance for me and never was. All I ended up getting was the shaft from all the team members protecting each others's fannies
. . . .

My team? We got postponed due to reign. R-e-i-g-n [she spelled it].

Shelter Problems

Grace (age 39, Los Angeles, California, 1987) had been to several shelters before I met her.

Yeah, I guess they all know me by now. It seems like they were happy to accept me and then I just sat there waiting for someone to help me get started again. But they were so busy doing nothing that I tried to go get jobs myself. And then they said I wasn't following their house rules. So I got kicked out.

After I'd been to one and admitted it, they checked-up on me and seemed to be just waiting for me to do something wrong. What could I do wrong? I just wanted to find a job and move out of there. Then when I hit the third shelter—in [another town]—one of the staff members really hated me and got nasty when I didn't do the chores she set out. So she must've gone down the line and told every shelter not to accept me anymore. Now they seem to see me coming and turn me down. And I may be the only one really trying to get ahead. I don't want their welfare. I want their help in getting a job.

I wonder how much work the staff is doing with the money they get to help women get on their feet again. If I'm any example, they just took the money and used it for a new TV.

In the Hometown "System"

Women often tell stories of being victimized by a family member and then by that person's influential political relatives. Marie (age 51, formerly from near St. Louis, Missouri, 1985) was married to a judge whose brother was the mayor of the town to which she escaped:

> It was wonderful when we had traffic tickets or something like that. It was rather fun to be the lady in the crowd who never had to worry about legal things. But then it all backfired. It wasn't fun to have to find a lawyer to go in front of the judge who took my husband's place on the bench for the day. What kind of fair play do you think I got?
>
> So I didn't get anything from the stand-in judge. Then I had to take care of the other house I owned—by myself from an inheritance—in a neighboring town where I moved after the divorce. I got a job, such as it was, to pay the taxes and such, and support myself, and it seemed that every month something else came up where I got in trouble with the law about the house. The fact that the mayor of the town was my husband's brother didn't have anything to do with it, right? Of course it did, and there wasn't anything to do but sell and get out. . . .
>
> And then the zoning board, all pals of the mayor, found that my house wasn't right by a foot or something, and I wasn't allowed to sell the house until I moved it. Can you imagine? Well, I couldn't, and I was finally served with some papers that said my neighbors, who, by the way, were related to one of the zoning board members, insisted that the house be torn down because it infringed on their property. After thirty-five years of no complaints! I don't even think any of it was the truth, but there wasn't anyone in town who would

listen to me; they were all bamboozled by the mayor and the zoning board.

I was forced to move out of the house, and along came heavy equipment and bounced the boards into the next county. I must have sat among the mess for days, and not one soul came up to me to help. I slept there until I was told to move off the property since it was being auctioned for taxes, and I don't even remember what happened during that period. I was in shock. But I know what I finally did: walk with my suitcases to the train station and sit there until I was put in jail as a loiterer. I stayed in jail for as long as I could. I didn't have any other place to go and I got free food. . . .

When I was told to leave, I was frightened. Where else could I go? It seemed to me that the only people who actually helped me at all were the police who gave me food and a bed. So do you know what I did? I stole a gun from a sporting goods store and held up the mayor and his wife in their house after I broke in. He had no choice but to have me arrested and put in jail, and after they let me go, I did it again, except that this time I held up the beauty parlor. Then I got a year. When I got out I held up the grocery store. I got three years. I think everyone in town knew what I was doing, and they must have had some pretty good laughs. When I was put out the last time, I was given a ticket to California, where I have a cousin who said she'd let me stay in her garage. Wonderful. I'm doing my research right now on how to get sent to the best prison in California. I'm not going to live and die on the streets out here. I'll be the only smart homeless woman, safe in a bed and with food and friends in a prison. Oh, I'm not kidding myself that it's going to be fun, but I'm going to write a book about it, and I'll just bet that the other women in the prison will all be on my side and I won't be beaten up or anything.

If you can't fight 'em, join 'em. I'm titling my book, *Pillow Politics*, and I'm going to get other stories from inmates about how they got snookered by politicians, hopefully relatives. I'm going to take off all the satin covers from the family beds and reveal political dirty linen.

In Private Lives and of Societal Issues

Family secrets often involve sensitive societal issues which bring community and judicial members into play. Helen (age 52, Los Angeles, California, 1986) lost her home, belongings, and bank account to the husband she protected from notoriety for twenty-one years. When he decided that it was safe for him to "come out of the closet" and bring his male lover into the house, Helen had a nervous breakdown and lost her job. She was in a support group when she told this story:

> For years he wouldn't let me even mention the word homosexual. None of our family friends would have believed me if I had said anything. Then came the '80s and it was "in" to admit that you belonged to the gay community. So he filed for a divorce and said I was cruel to him because of his homosexuality. What a lie! He had treated me like shit for years because all he wanted out of a marriage was a cover-up to keep his big career going. . . .

> His lawyer was gay. The judge was gay. My lawyer was stupid enough to say it out loud and ask for another judge. Guess who got the house and everything in it! You just can't break up the gay community in California; they stick together like glue. . . .

> When I got out of the hospital [from the nervous breakdown] my ex-husband practically threw me out when I tried to get my clothes from my room. Do you know that his boyfriend had worn some of my things and the seams were all torn out? His sweat smell was on them, too. It certainly wasn't mine! How could I appear calm and in command of myself after that? I went for a couple of job interviews and

ended up crying in the waiting room. If it weren't for Betty here, I'd be roaming the freeways looking for a bus to fling myself under. . . .

No one wants to admit how much power the gays and lesbians have in California. It's a political thing, too. If you dare say someone is gay, it's taken as a slap of discrimination. A person can get elected just by saying he's gay or she's a lesbian. I'm not supposed to be upset because my husband preferred another guy to me—and then got everything I owned because there is more compassion for the gays than the married woman.

In the Matter of the Powerless

While many homeless women carry letters, bills, photos, affidavits, and other evidence which provides proof in part of what they proclaim—collusive and/or corruptive behavior by those in social, legal, and political power—it is highly unlikely that they will ever gain entrance to the judicial system for indemnification. It is difficult enough for those who are relatively healthy, housed, fed, and mentally strong to "fight the system." I know. I tried for several years to gain access to the Maryland court system just so I could testify against an abusive husband, his attorneys (one of whom had possession of the gun used against me by my husband), a court clerk, the Bar Association which protected its own from investigation, and a slew of public officials who ignored what is indisputably a criminal act: an intentional lie on an official court paper to keep a battered woman from appearing at her own trial (see Appendix).

I had to give up when the statute of limitations ran out. I know that our stories sound unbelievable; this is America, after all. But I do not raise my eyebrows when I hear pre-homeless and homeless women explaining experiences that appear outlandish. I know it as fact that if a woman cannot afford a private attorney to fight for her in court, she has no chance of ever obtaining indemnification— whether it be related to a workingplace, organizational, media, system, or family matter. (The only *pro bono* [free] legal activity I have heard of has had immense publicity value.) To attempt to act as one's own attorney (*pro per* or *pro se*) takes ability, time, and money; it is not an activity open to women who must expend their energies on daily sustaining shelter, food, and sanity. Because of the large number of homeless women who correlate injustice with experiences involving government-regulated systems, the next chapter will address public sector policy and practices.

Chapter Four

Blind [In]justice and Social [Ir]responsibility

When homeless women discuss their lives and losses, our legal, judicial, welfare, and Social Security systems come under intense scrutiny. What results is the realization that our public policies and services are not necessarily correlated with social responsibility: attention to human desires, needs, and rights. There are serious inadequacies, omissions, and mismanagements attendant to the services that are often proudly proclaimed by governmental sources as "efficient" and "committed." Those who are victimized doubt that there is any such thing as "social justice"; they rename everything connected with "justice" to "injustice," the most popular references directed at our civil and criminal [in]justice systems.

Even when policy seems to be correlated with a solution to a problem, the inconsistencies caused by the lack of service connections result in so many cracks that virtually everyone must deal with an entanglement of service provider agencies, public offices and programs, and court-related systems. Women who have been victims of domestic abuse, for example, often partake of shelter services while also being directed to social welfare agencies, legal aid bureaus, police stations, courthouse personnel, counselors, and a multiple of related referrals—and *still* end up on the streets. Each system has faults. Together, systems do not conjoin to meet the needs of pre-homeless women.

1. The Legal System

Legal Aid, Lawyer's Referral, and Volunteer Agencies

There is nothing that Legal Aid will do for the married woman who needs representation in court for a divorce—unless there is an important child custody problem that appeals to the particular office. The vast majority of women, therefore, who *must* obtain alimony and tangibles to survive are turned away by the largest legal agency which is funded to assist the poor. Legal Aid usually suggests that poor women needing representation for domestic relief get a referral from the Bar Association's Lawyer Referral Service. I have not heard of one case yet wherein any lawyer responded as willing to represent an indigent female who might never be able to pay. In major cities there are usually other agencies which claim to supply no-fee lawyers to appropriate clients. However, battered housewives, live-in partners, and homeless women are rarely if ever "appropriate" clients. Even when a lawyer volunteers to represent someone in court, that does not mean that there is nothing to be paid by the client. There are investigative costs, filing and other court fees, service charges, and the hidden costs of transportation, parking, telephone calls, and often child care and suitable clothing. Homeless women cannot meet the "rules of the game."

Terry (age 55, Baltimore, Maryland, 1979) had a typical experience with Legal Aid and the "volunteer" lawyers:

> I tell you I've never had the shakes like when I left that office. I was so mad. . . .

> Here I tell the lawyer that I got a nice house in both our names and I got to get a divorce because he's always beating me up. He tells me they don't take on divorce cases. So what *do* you take on, I asked. He just gave me that look that says you're worth nothing and turned away to clip his nails
> . . . .

> I finally just had to pick up and leave everything that was mine. I couldn't get the police to do anything since Hank

didn't leave any marks on me. Kidney damage doesn't show.

I lived in my car right behind the Legal Aid Office building for two weeks, going in every day to beg for help. One guy finally told me to go over to the Bar Association's office for a referral to a regular lawyer.

Do you believe me when I tell you that they never had one lawyer to refer me to. . . . I thought for awhile that I'd gotten a lawyer through an agency which says it has volunteer lawyers for free. But then the guy starts listing all the fees I got to pay. I told him if I had all that money, I wouldn't be sittin' in his office! He almost threw me out. . . .

So my husband got my house and everything else and said I had abandoned him. He had a lawyer paid for with our bank account—which he got to first. I wouldn't even have known he got the divorce except that I seen it in a newspaper column listing about divorces granted. . . .

Immigration Problems

Immigrant women find themselves forced to interact with federal, state, and local offices which deal with residential status while also needing the services of attorneys, adult and child welfare workers, housing officials, employers and employment agencies, and a myriad of allied programs which may entail the use of interpreters. Illegal aliens often endure years of physical pain and psychological torture because complaints may lead to detention and/or deportation. Felice (age 38, Los Angeles, California, 1987) tells us that just finding an attorney who understands immigration law is difficult:

I not able to do these things that your office says I must. I not have a house to stay in and I must find work right away. No one has any for me. How do I get to these places that I have to make papers for? Do you give bus fare? I not have a car. . . .

I will be taken to deportation center if I not get lawyer and into court. I go—went—to immigration lawyer and he charge. I go, ah, to Legalization Office and I told I no have right forms and so go to other office and told I have to prove why I here. How? I told to prove how I here, what I do here, too. What can I prove when I alone and taking care of myself? Nobody understand my country. . . .

How I get immigration lawyer who knows what I—what problems I have? No one know how I must—what I must do to live the way I should. I not grow up like you are.

Members of particular populations (notably Pacific-Asian) may still be bound by tradition/culture so as to remain silent about family violence; shame in reportage is dreaded more than beatings. Second and third generation women may retain those cultural standards even though they express "assimilation" in many other areas of daily life. Lee (age 29, San Francisco, California, 1984) had been in the United States for three years when one of her relatives called a shelter to see if there was any money available for battered women.

My cousin has brought shame to me and my family by calling and telling people what has happened to me. It is such shame that I should not be forgiven by my ancestors, and rightfully I should die. I and my ancestors grieve. The idea that I should sue my husband is beyond what I can understand. I cannot put that added shame onto my whole family. . . .

I only came to live with these cousins because my husband beat me every night when he came home full of drugs. He wanted me to act like a loving wife and make him feel good, but he beat me while I am serving him. So my cousin saw my bruises and demanded that he stop. He got mad and put me out of the door. I do not have a home anymore. She brought me to Los Angeles to live with her and is trying to get him to let me go to someone else, but I am not good for anyone else now; I am used. I will not be accepted by any other decent man, so I never will have a home of my own again. I cannot even go back to China.

I am shamed forever, and I just wait for death.

The cultural aspects of social responsibility seem to be neglected across the board. In a pluralistic society which claims to be advanced, we lack support groups which cater to particular racial and ethnic needs and interests. I tried to create such support groups at a shelter for battered women and for the City Attorney's Office. Neither publicly-funded "agency" was interested in instituting cultural awareness sessions.

Transgressions by Attorneys

Misconduct by members of the legal profession and the boards which monitor them is not a matter of secrecy; two of the states in which I have interviewed extensively are attempting to address the problem. In California, a 1987 report endorsed by Attorney General John Van de Kamp points to the inaccessability of the public to the disciplinary procedure of the State Bar Association and a related problem within the Bar itself to uncover incompetent lawyers. Van de Kamp referred to the current disciplinary system in analogy to a Rube Goldberg procedure. Monitor Robert Fellmeth, who conducted the investigation, criticized the Bar for neither discovering nor preventing improper behavior of lawyers. In addition, Fellmeth found that only an aggressive and articulate (alleged) victim of an attorney might stand a chance of having his or her case being considered for initial acceptance. This admission of attorney malfeasance and/or nonfeasance is also suggested by the Maryland Court of Appeals in its appointment of a committee to study the American Bar Association Model Rules of Professional Conduct (1983). That committee recommended changes in the standards for ethical conduct for Maryland lawyers (1985), but nothing has changed victims' access to the disciplinary procedure—which is totally within the control of an autonomous unit: the Attorney Grievance Commission (staffed by attorneys). A victim's only alternative is to hire an attorney to try individual cases of malfeasance at the district court level. This is obviously an impossibility for impoverished and homeless women, especially in light of the massive cutbacks in legal aid services.

Jennine (age 58, Baltimore, Maryland, 1979) relates details which are all too familiar:

> I really suffered through that marriage. I mean, he treated me worse than any wife deserves. . . he set up rules and regulations for me to follow, and punished me when I didn't obey. When I finally insisted that I was going to get a divorce, he said we couldn't afford two lawyers, and we went to someone he knew.
>
> The lawyer said he would represent us both so we'd save money. I believed him, and I thought he was representing my interests. But then I was given papers to sign which I didn't like. I got practically nothing. The lawyer told me that was more than I'd ever get from a judge. I tried to tell him that I couldn't live on that little bit, but eventually I did sign. I found out later, after I'd gone broke in only a year of living like a pauper, that a lawyer in Maryland isn't even allowed to represent both parties. There wasn't anything I could do about it. I couldn't hire another lawyer. I couldn't reach anyone to complain about it.

2. The Judicial System

While our Constitution requires that all people accused of a crime shall have free legal representation, there is no provision for free legal assistance to or trials on behalf of the victims. Consequently, there are no civil trials unless the victim can afford to retain a private attorney (discounting an attempt to represent oneself) or the case is so unusual or sensational that a lawyer is willing to accept it without a fee. (Obviously there are alternatives to legal fees: media coverage, creating a landmark case, and advancing personal reputation.)

Therefore, anyone who has been arrested and cannot afford a private attorney automatically receives the services of a public defender. However, if an indigent woman is the *victim*, she is provided with free legal assistance *only* if the *state* files charges against her abuser. The prosecuting attorney is only representing the people of the state and their interest in controlling unacceptable behavior. *The victim's* interests may be left by the proverbial wayside even if the abuser is admonished or jailed. Sometimes a woman retaliates against abuse and ends up being punished herself—by the courts and society—while the initial offender walks away smiling.

Criminal Actions Calling for Civil Suits

Stephanie (age 49, Los Angeles, California, 1985) attempted to murder an abuser who held her a sexual captive. The only real reason that her story has been heard is because of prurient interest:

> I lost almost ten years of my life because I went nuts and tried to get even with the guy who ruined my body and fucked up my mind. You'd think some psychiatrist would understand, but no, everyone said I had to pay a debt to society. The asshole who kept me tied up in his car for a week and made me do all kinds of awful things to him while he got money from men to watch us—he got a suspended sentence because I broke his legs. He was going to be put away for a while but he never did have to go to jail because he had a damn good lawyer who got him off on a technicality. It's a shame that my public defender wasn't as good a lawyer. And I don't think he really cared what happened to a woman.
>
> So now I got no place to go and no one will hire me for anything. My mind is still in a fog somewhere. I keep having nightmares about all the men watching me do humiliating things to that guy. And I'll never forget the smell in that car after I'd been kept there for an entire week. I wish I had killed the son of a bitch. At least I'd feel that I got rid of some of my problems.

I tried to get a civil trial going against that lizard; he's loaded. No lawyer would take it for free. Where do they think I'm going to get any money if no one will hire me because my life is so ruined that I can't even hold a decent conversation, let alone a job of any kind? So here I am, walking the streets and talking to just about anyone who'll listen— and lots do since it's about sex, but half of them think I'm nuts. I guess I am, but what happened to me is the truth and if I can't get into the court system, I got no future. I had to pay for being tortured. He won't even have to go to court to explain why he did it.

While Stephanie participated in a criminal action, she blames attorney incompetence and lack of understanding for her loss. It is quite obvious that Stephanie has serious problems which are not going to be *cured* by entry into the court system with a civil suit against her abuser. However, it is also quite clear that she needs assistance, closure, and indemnification. Winning a (civil) lawsuit against the man would provide some personal gratification—along with money to live on and pay for the psychotherapy which she needs (and cannot obtain in a free clinic). In continuing storytellings Stephanie reconstructed how the abuser was able to hire an attorney with an excellent reputation for "getting criminals off" (her words) in conjunction with the injustices involved regarding gender and career opportunities. She characterized at length her lack of an advanced education and consequent minimum wage jobs which kept her trapped in an economic and social vise. "If I'd had the chance for a decent career like men do," she stated, "I'd have been able to hire a good private lawyer too."

Unclear Charges and Representation

Jackie (age 59, Baltimore, Maryland, 1978) was living in a shed which hid a commercial trash bin when I met her strictly by accident: I was looking for a ring which I lost during lunch, and had been directed to the trash in the back of the small mall. I opened the doors which surrounded the bin, and Jackie was leaning against the side of the shed, trying to get the heavy white plastic "tag" off of a skirt which was undoubtedly stolen from a store. We were both taken aback. She did not try to hide the skirt. I pretended that I did not see it. I apologized for frightening her and explained that the manager of the restaurant had instructed me to look in the trash for my lost ring. (We talked and looked for about half an hour, and I asked her if I could return later with a Chinese take-out dinner and record her story. She agreed.)

Typical, isn't it? Men are always telling us what to do. Now, if he were really a good manager, he would have had one of the help come with you and do the dirty work of looking through this stuff. [She got up and dusted herself off.] Well, honey, *I'll* help you look. Just because I make a couple of bucks an hour instead of twenty doesn't mean that I'm any less of a person. [The rest of the following story was recorded later.]

I had a house of my own just a few years ago. And a husband. But he died, I had to sell the house for nothing just to pay his debts, and then I went to live with an uncle. Well, he went on and on about my going to work, and I tried, but I wasn't young then and no one wanted me. Besides, I didn't have any formal education beyond high school. When I was young we were supposed to go to work as a secretary or get married. I couldn't get the hang of shorthand, so I ended up in a dime store, clerking.

My uncle died about three years after I moved in, and the police kept questioning me about the way he died. They thought I did something to him. Do you know that after all this time I still don't know how I'm supposed to have killed him? It's the truth. The police just kept asking me stupid questions, and I guess I answered wrong. Anyway, I was arrested and put in jail for the longest time. I nearly went mad because I hadn't done nothing wrong. It seemed like they just locked the door and forgot about me. Finally, I was put in the courtroom and some fancy attorney for my uncle's estate brought up how I was just living off of him and was waiting for my inheritance, and killed him for it. I didn't even know I was going to get an inheritance from him! I guess I had someone speaking for me, but I'm darned if I know who it was. It seemed like this fancy attorney just was in charge of everything, and then every once in a while a cop said something, and then the coroner said something, and then the judge had little chats up at his desk with the fancy guy and someone who I suppose was representing me, but there wasn't any real personal contact. See, I guess they really didn't have any evidence at all that I'd done anything to my uncle. It was like an old-fashioned farce movie. When I tried to ask what was going on, no one would tell me. I was shushed and made to feel like it wasn't my life that was on the line. . . .

So they never did really have a trial the way I know them from the Perry Masons. I think they just had to let me go after that first courtroom thing. I never wished I'd had an education more than then. I had no idea of what was going on, and if I had been smarter, I might have gotten out of jail and then gotten the inheritance which was supposed to be mine. But when I tried to get a lawyer after they let me out, I was practically given the heave ho from every legal office I went into. I was a joke. Men, now, they wouldn't be put in that position. They all get some chances to do something even if they aren't smart. Someone gives them a job, they move up and soon have a lifetime career. Me, I never had a chance at all. I'm lucky to work as a cleaning lady in an office building. For just enough to buy some food and stay sane. But I sleep here—on a mat I keep clean in the office building—and I spend any free time wandering around the park and looking for clothes and such. How I wish I'd been born a stupid man and gotten a career. . . .

It is not clear whether Jackie was involved in a trial or simply appeared in a pre-trial hearing or an arraignment court. She certainly was a silent stakeholder in the judicial process, a situation in which too many abused women find themselves.

Inadequate Representation

Other women discuss participation in terms of "Is that *my* lawyer?" Rhonda (age 39, Baltimore, Maryland, 1978) expresses outrage whenever attorneys are mentioned:

> I know that I couldn't afford to have the best, but I think I could have had someone who was alive! There he was, all limpy and so nervous, and maybe I was his first case or something, but you'd think the judge would notice that and let him off for the day. . . .

> I told him all about being taken for all my money by a man I know lives in Catonsville. I saw him shopping in stores there before and after he got my money. I heard the cops call it a scam, and they had a funny name for it like they knew all about that kind of thing. So here's my lawyer listening to the charges against me—assault and battery and a few other big words for hitting the guy in the groin with my boot and chasing him into a store and screaming that he was a thief and someone should topple him—and he doesn't even let me explain why I did it.

> The trial took a day and a half, and then the lawyers huddled in front of the judge like it was a football game, and then my lawyer comes back to our table and says it's all over and I'm going to be let go. Well, I says, what about that scumball? Don't I get to tell what he did and I should get my money back? He just clicked his briefcase shut and said that was not important! I mean, hell; why did he listen to why I clobbered the scumball and why was I let off if it wasn't important? He got every penny I had in the world! What was he doing there, anyway? Wasn't he supposed to be helping me? Oh, I know; I guess I sound foolish. I was expecting to get what was mine back, and all that happened was that I didn't have to go to jail and the bum walked. . . .

> I tried to get other people in the courthouse to do something about that man, but all I ever heard was that the case was

closed. Now I'm out in the cold and the scumball is living off of my $26,000. What was that limpy man doing for me? Or wasn't he really meant to be my attorney at all? I'm glad I'm not in jail, but that wasn't the point at all!

Personal (*Pro Per*) Representation

Doris (age 49, Baltimore, Maryland, 1979) refused to accept being told that she was "a loser" (her words) and decided that she would represent herself in court. She found that acting on one's own behalf has drawbacks:

They thought they'd put every obstacle in my way so that I couldn't make it into the courtroom. But I fooled them. I filled out all the proper papers, even though they made me do them time and time again. No one was willing to help me. Then I couldn't get anyone to serve Jim, so I struck a bargain with a man who could manage it. Don't ask me what I had to do in return. . . .

I was treated like a second class citizen from the minute we got into the courtroom. This frozen-faced judge just looked at me and I could see him trying to think of ways to make me miserable. Well, he found them all. Every time I said something, he reminded me I should have had an attorney because my questioning or responses were improper. I told him I couldn't find a lawyer a hundred times, but he didn't even listen to me. Jim had an attorney, and he sure did make mincemeat out of me; if I said something, he objected and it was sustained. When he said something that I thought was completely out of line, I objected and it was overruled. The judge kept warning me about procedure. He really didn't care about facts at all. Finally, he called a recess and went off to think about it, I guess. When he came back, he told me I handled myself unprofessionally and didn't make my case properly—while he praised Jim's attorney for being so patient with me. Jim never had to say a word, of course. And then the judge said he was dismissing the case and I had better watch out about what I said about people. I really needed a chewing-out in public. . . .

People in the audience said I had done a good job, and everyone believed me. They said he [the judge] was just angry because I tried to be my own lawyer. In the hallway I heard that he hated women and even female lawyers hated to come up in front of him. Just my luck. . . .

So even though everyone knows that I was conned and had every penny taken away from me illegally, I lost my case because of my lack of proper courtroom procedure. I'd like to force the judge to go buy a bra in a women's store where all the saleswomen have been screwed by a man.

Complicated Representation

Child custody cases are no less difficult to pursue when an attorney cannot be located to file papers and represent the female client. Gail (age 24, Los Angeles, California, 1987) filed charges of wife abuse against her husband, had a (criminal branch) hearing in which it was revealed that the child had also been injured by her father, and eventually he was convicted of spouse abuse (after intrial plea bargaining released him from other criminal charges). Because Gail had had to flee to another state to save her life and protect her child from harm, she was also involved in a child custody problem which eventually spanned two state systems. Intermittently she and the child were without a home, alternating refuge with relatives and friends. The attorney representing the state (California) for the criminal branch denied that Gail's abuse and the child's welfare were conjoined issues. As a result, only the civil court could play a part in determining the child's future, and it was determined that the abuser was perfectly suitable as a half-year father. Consequently, the civil court system showed no mercy when it came to expecting Gail (a penniless victim) to commute to California at the husband's demand. When she tried to change the jurisdiction for the child custody hearings, she found that she had to have attorneys in both states despite the fact that she could not afford any at all. Finally, a commissioner for the (California) civil court issued a bench warrant for Gail's arrest because she did not arrive in time for yet another hearing to determine custody. No one considered the victim's financial needs—or the child's situation. No one in the legal system was interested in the fact that Gail and her child were periodically homeless as a direct result of domestic violence.

I just don't understand it. There is no question that my husband beat me unmercifully over a period of years. There are medical and hospital reports all over the place. In every story I told [to the criminal branch attorneys] there were references to how he also hit [the child] and threatened to take her away from me. There are witnesses to everything. He tried to kill her before she was born by punching me in the stomach late in my pregnancy. He told a number of people that he only married me to get citizenship, and he certainly didn't want a child. And yet when I took the child to another state to keep us both safe, I ended up being told that I had no right to do that.

Why can't everyone see that the child and I are part of the same problem, that being the physical and psychological abuse heaped on us by my husband? Why do I have to defend myself when I am the victim? Everything in the system seems to be against me and the child and giving every opportunity and right to our abuser. I'm terrified of him, can't afford to keep coming back to California, and have to hide when I do. Does everyone think that airplane tickets and housing are free? And what am I supposed to do with the child when I'm afraid to bring her to California? Who is going to pay for her care while I am going back and forth?. . . .

There is something terribly wrong when no one understands that the child's welfare is attached to mine and the courts separate abuse into criminal and civil matters. It is all one case, and just because I can't afford lawyers for the civil case, I end up victimized again. The whole thing is a nightmare. Why aren't there lawyers to represent us in the civil case when a convicted abuser is able to afford a lawyer to demand my presence here and I can't afford to come? Now there's a warrant out for my arrest if I show up in California!

Voluntary Courtroom Testimony

Battered women often volunteer to testify against abusers. This is especially so in the case of attacks which have escalated from slaps to broken bones and permanent injuries. Maria (age 39, Los Angeles, California, 1987) had testified against her husband after relatives had told her not to call them again if she did not act positively to halt her husband's violence. (The family was just as fed up with Maria as with the abuser, a response common in domestic violence cases: relatives and friends become annoyed with the victim.) She called the City Attorney's Office long after the file had been closed to ask for a referral to a shelter for battered women. I explained that she was not a candidate for such a shelter since she had not been living with or been abused by her husband for over a year. She was now simply a homeless woman.

But I cooperated with the City Attorney's Office by testifying! I didn't really want to at first, but the prosecutor talked me into it. He said nothing would ever change for me. My life would always be a hell. Well, he certainly didn't say I was going to become homeless! This *is* hell!

You know, I was better off when I was being hit all the time. At least I had a home. After Thomas got out of custody, he was angrier than the devil himself and slapped me around again. He said that if I called the police he would kill me. The judge had told him that he could go to counseling for batterers and I knew it wouldn't do any good, and I was right. He just laughed his way through the few weeks and came at me with a bat when it was over. So I called the cops from the hospital, and they put him in jail and he got a month or so. You know he treated me worse when he got out. . . .

So I had a choice of staying with him and being treated the same way or moving out into the street. The city attorney didn't care about that. All he cared about was making sure he looked good by prosecuting my husband. Big deal. Now he's beating on some other woman, but she's got a roof over her head. What's the point of my testifying if I'm the one who suffers?

Involuntary Courtroom Testimony

Other women are "threatened" and practically forced by the state to testify against an abuser. Renee (age 34, Los Angeles, California, 1987) explains the procedure and its ramifications:

I didn't want to testify against John. I knew from previous experience that if I did anything against him I'd be the worse for it. So after I'd called the police and made the report, I tried to get him out of jail and cancel the whole thing. But a city attorney called me and said that I had to testify because he had a record of beating me up and this time he wasn't going to get away with it.

I said I wouldn't do it because I knew it would go worse for me. The city attorney threatened me. He said, "I'll haul you into court with a subpoena and you'll have to testify or go to jail yourself." He was scary. I mean, that's not right. He's supposed to care what happens to me. There's no other place for me and the kids to go, and he wasn't giving me any money or house to live in. . . .

So I came in with the kids and sat there all morning and finally was called. I was too afraid not to tell what happened, and John got sent to county jail for a while, but I had to get out before he did. He would have killed us. So the kids are living with some relatives, and I am going from one mission to another hoping that someone will hire me as a live-in maid. I don't know when I'll ever get to live with the kids again, and I don't know how long the relatives will keep them. It's awful. I should have been allowed to drop the charges if I decided that it was the best thing for me and the kids. Now I am in a worse spot.

Special Problems of the Immigrant Woman

The immigrant woman is in a particularly difficult position if the police submit a violence report which is filed in the judiciary system. Maria (age 41, Los Angeles, California, 1987) requested that charges be dropped against her abusive husband.

> I didn't call the police. My neighbors did when they heard me screaming. I told the police that I was okay, but they saw the blood and took Jorge into custody. I don't want no trouble with the police, and I want to drop all the charges against him. If I don't have him to live with, what am I supposed to do? I can't get a job with all these kids, and we have to eat. Am I just supposed to go and find another man who will take us in? What makes you think that he will treat us better? Don't you know that Mexican men grow up treating women like animals? We don't get the respect that you American women get. . . we're just belongings to Mexican men.

If an immigrant woman is also an illegal alien, her fate is worse if she becomes involved in the court system. Anna (age 43, Santa Monica, California, 1987) pleaded to have her husband released from jail before his arraignment court appearance:

> You don't understand what will happen to me if Julio goes into court and maybe gets jail. I didn't want that. I didn't mean for the police to put him in there. I can't let anything happen to Julio. If he doesn't want me any more, it means that I have to go back to Mexico, and I didn't have any life there. I know that if he doesn't forgive me for this I will have to go to the streets right away, and then immigration will take me away. Julio was in trouble last year and I had to go to the streets for two months. I was treated worse by the men who didn't give me a bed and toilet inside a house. . . .
>
> It took me years to get here, and I'm willing to let him get drunk and hit me if it means I can stay in U.S. Maybe I'll

win the lottery and I'll have a life somewhere without Julio,
but until then I just want to hide.

3. The Social Welfare System
Public Assistance

It is not uncommon for homeless women to be eligible for public
assistance and either not realize it or refuse to follow through with
the proper procedures to obtain General Relief checks, food stamps,
vouchers for motels, and state-paid medical aid. The women whose
lives and stories are presented in this book are not those who would
normally go to an office or hotel/motel in a "bad area." They also
prefer to live by strategy rather than pursue what they perceive to
be degrading experiences: spending days standing in long lines
with people they know or assume are dirty, answering embarrassing, personal questions about their backgrounds and resources, and
using food stamps which pinpoint them as "poor." Further, the
public assistance programs are almost all county-run (even though
administration and funding may involve federal and state sponsorship) and the inconsistencies of requirements even intrastate make
application and aid procedures frustrating and often not worthwhile. Becky (age 58, Los Angeles, California, 1988) expresses how
she feels about the local programs:

> Listen, at first I tried to do it the regular way. I went to the
> wrong offices—spent hours on buses to get there—and was
> treated like an animal in a vet hospital. Why wasn't I in my
> own area?, the intake lady asked. And why didn't I have
> any ID? And why did I say I had no resources when I had a
> car worth $4000? Sell it, she said, and we'll give you $319 a
> month to live on. Are they crazy or something? Where am I
> going to stay for maybe $200 a month—without utilities? In
> Skid Row hotels, she said.

> Hah! I'm better off in my car on a side street near Beverly
> Hills! So I'd get food stamps. Okay. But I eat just fine in the
> grocery stores and in the happy-hour bars. And if I need to
> go to the hospital, then I'll go into the emergency room and

take my chances. I can always give a phony address. The whole thing was disgusting. . . .

Cynthia (age 61, Santa Monica, California, 1988) complains that the system makes one completely dependent on one state—and indeed, often one city—for survival.

When I got relief checks for a year, I was tied to the area. I was always waiting to go to an office for something. I didn't want to stay in that awful neighborhood, but otherwise I'd have to live on buses. . . .

I tried to change my relief office and got such a fuss. More papers to fill out, and more interviews so's they could try to find some motel that didn't have lice. And the food stamps always ran out before the month did. . . .

I'm telling you, I had a much better time of it when I got on my own and could travel around and look out for myself. I changed states three times to check out how I could live better. Some places got real good malls to spend the day in, and other places got cheap movie houses where I can eat popcorn and candy bars by using what money I can find or steal, and by now I know how to be self-reliant. I'm not going to get tied to any system stuff again. . . .

I'm not going to be one of those women you see sitting by her pushcart in rags a'mumbling to herself. No ma'am. I look pretty good and I can move right along with the crowd and no one stares at poor ol' me.

4. The Social Security System

Survivors and Disability Insurance

There is such misunderstanding about who can receive benefits that one wonders where women get so much misinformation. At first I thought that women were just "passing gossip" and believed what they heard without questioning it. But after many interviews, I realized that a great deal of misinformation comes directly from the Social Security offices—the main one in Baltimore and the local branches throughout the country. The stories that homeless women tell reveal that perhaps half could be receiving monthly checks that would make a significant difference in their lifestyles. Widows usually are aware of their husbands' Social Security benefits, but separated and divorced women are generally unaware of payments for which they may apply. Sophia (age 58, Los Angeles, California, 1988) provides us with information about *three* very important guidelines for monthly support:

> When I left home, well, when Paul made it plain that I couldn't stay, I just sort of wandered for awhile. I knew my money was going to run out, and even though I knew I couldn't hold a job, I tried to get one. I can't really do anything because of my arthritis [she uses crutches] and besides, I'd been just taking care of my house for my whole marriage. Not that it was that long. It was my second time around, and we'd only been married for eight years. Now I was married to Tom, my first husband, for seventeen years. . . .
>
> I thought I'd ask about some sort of government help, but I figured I wouldn't get anything until I was 62. And I had only been married for eight years, and one of the Social Security ladies told me I'd have had to been married for ten years. Since Tom is still working and has another wife, I can't get anything from him, and so I guess I'll never get any Social Security at all. . . since I'm never going to make it to 62 anyway. . . .

Sophia had been informed incorrectly. First of all, she *had* been married to Paul for ten years because I discovered that he did not file for a divorce until *eleven* years after the date of their marriage! Even though they separated after eight years, the determinant of "years of marriage" is from the date of marriage until the date of the final divorce decree! Secondly, Sophia is classified as a "surviving divorced spouse" since Paul had died since the divorce, and Sophia could receive benefits at age *60*. *However*, since she had been disabled before he died (the rule is that she must have been disabled before his death *or* no later than seven years after his death), Sophia would be eligible for benefits at age 50 (assuming that Paul was deceased at that time).

The intricacies of the Social Security system have kept many women from realizing financial support that would mean the difference between having a "house" and living in a car. Andrea (age 64, San Diego, California, 1986) could be a "surviving divorced spouse"; she assumes that she is not eligible for any benefits because she remarried after her divorce from Grant:

> My second marriage hasn't been all that great, and I'm sorry I ever got into this mess. I wouldn't have to be thinking about living on the skids if I'd just stayed married to Grant. He died a couple of years after our divorce, and I'd be getting his Social Security payments if I hadn't married Peter. What a fool I was.
>
> I married again just so's I'd have someone to talk to, and Peter won't even say a word. He just sits around with his buddies and drinks up what he makes. We haven't had a decent day's interest in each other since our honeymoon.
>
> I guess I'm being punished. What I'd give to go back to the day before I married again. . . .

Andrea's remarriage does not preclude her from divorcing Peter and being reinstated as Grant's beneficiary. If she married Peter before she was 60, her benefits will begin starting with the month of her divorce.

Other Benefits

There are, of course, many other circumstances wherein a woman may receive money from Social Security, Medicare, Medicaid, Railroad Retirement, Supplemental Security Income, Unemployment Insurance, state supplements of SSI, child support, Worker's Compensation, and veterans, government employees, and miners benefits. I usually carry the Social Security Handbook (purchased from the Government Printing Office for approximately $13) for general information on the variety of possible payments for which a homeless woman may be eligible. However, each state has different coverage and it is necessary to address needs and assistance on a state-by-state basis.

Given that most homeless women are not utilizing the public sector systems to their advantage or have been victimized by the individuals who work for those systems (or the regulations which are the systems), we can correctly assume that "justice" and "social responsibility" should be expanded to include the examination of and solutions to the problems which women explicate.

The stresses of pre-homeless and homeless life must have particular effects on physical and mental health. What events are implicated and what manifestations are correlated? Read on. . . .

Chapter Five

The Ragged Edge of Sanity

Many homeless women have long histories of mental illness, have been irresponsibly or inadvertantly released from mental institutions and do roam the streets in a virtual daze. Other women suffer psychological deterioration as a direct result of street living after either a landslide effect of personal devastation or "overnight indigency." And there are those who are prime candidates for mental illness because of past trauma which only needs exacerbation. The women whose stories are included in this book are *not* those who are dysfunctionally mentally ill and need to be institutionalized, and I base that evaluation on their ability to strategically manage their lives in private and public settings: they are self-reliant; not physically identifiable as homeless; do not aim loud, illogical speech at the general populace; and do not exist in psychological isolation (in which there is total silence and an apparent lack of awareness of others). That does not mean that anger, hostility, and fears do not occasionally overwhelm a generally calm exterior or that personal demons do not haunt the recesses of the mind. Personal stories reveal experiences which can be identified as causing some measure of psychic disturbance in the spectrum of "mental health." Beliefs and behaviors are affected. Manifestations include explications of traditional phenomena (such as a nighttime attack by "The Old Hag"), religious visitations, extraterrestrial sightings/meetings, and out-of-body and near-death experiences as well as phobic and compulsive activities.

Professionals have been quick to label peculiar behavior and expressions of the aberrant as mental illness. Are we to ignore the importance of catharsis and the cutting edge of therapeutics? Is it not possible that a supranormal religious encounter is a coping mechanism to deal with spiritual need and a prelude to social and church activity? Cannot a "hagging" attack denote the acceptance and integration of abuse into one's life experiences to balance and perpetuate personhood? We can defy prevalent attitudes and seek the meanings and functions of themes and motifs which are repeated as (concretized and symbolic) scripts and performances. These dramatic representations (storytellings, nightmares, daydreams, and hallucinations) provide an acceptable outlet for unacceptable public behavior, revealing emotions which are repressed and deniable as well as overt wish fulfillments.

1. Compulsive Behavior

Repeated Behavior

Dorothy (age 59, Los Angeles, California, 1987) was observed going up and down the escalator in a mall twice in each direction before settling on one level. I stood behind her (and her three large bags) as she repeated the action. She was mumbling about the elevator, and I asked her if it was out of order.

> Got to do this again. . . yes, just once. Only once. Not twice. One more time and then it will be twice. . . See, if you go up twice you are safe on that level. Got to concentrate on what's safe now. How to stay. . . Did you ever think how it is to be stuck between two floors? You're nowhere. But you're trapped at somewhere. Remember Winnie the Pooh? Not safe, not safe.

I got off at the next level and immediately wrote (as accurately as possible) her commentary into a notebook. I do not understand the reference to Winnie the Pooh, but obviously it has some meaning to Dorothy. She was a recent addition to the "mall women" and I had not noticed the up-and-down syndrome before, although I had spoken to her a few times after seeing her taking bagged food-for-the-trash which is left behind the carry-out food stalls. (Naturally I never told her I saw such activity. It simply verified my opinion that she was a homeless woman moving into the mall.) One story related by Dorothy referred to her previous employment.

> I was working for the May Company. Yes, right over there. I guess I wasn't very good. They moved me from one floor to another, to one department after another. . . It was like being pushed and pulled and I was so unsure of myself. I began to get scared when I came in in the morning. Where would they put me next? I was a nervous wreck, and I wasn't used to doing stand-up work, and my legs bothered me. I had a good office job [before that] until my boss let me go. I couldn't understand why. I was a good typist, and I thought I'd be a lifetime employee.

> But you know how it is—when you get older. I stopped by the office a few weeks later and my desk was being used by a pretty young thing who was pecking away at the typewriter with one finger on the erase switch. . . .

> It was hard to get anything, but I ended up at the May Company and thought I might move up to something better than being on my feet all day. It just didn't work out. . . . Then I had to move from my room—the lady who rented it sold the house—and I couldn't find anything I could afford. It all happened so fast that I didn't realize that I didn't have a place to stay, and I remembered that I could stay the day in this mall, so I just came here. . . . I've been here, um, ah, [she figured on her fingers] five weeks now. I've applied for unemployment, but I don't know. . . they've put me off twice now. If I don't qualify, I don't know what I'll do. . . .

Dorothy's up-and-down safety measures are probably symbolic of her constant movement from one department and floor to another, and reflect the uncertainty/fear of her future and safety in continuity. In any case, the repeated behavior which she employs calms her; there is no doubt that she is suffering psychic distress; but is she "mentally ill"? I do not think so.

Sonia (age 67, Hollywood, California, 1983) focused on the repeated checking of her car while we were talking in a small park; she would rise suddenly, walk a few steps to stare at it, and then return to our bench. She did this many times within a half hour or so.

> I just know someone is going to steal my stuff. It's all good, you know. I spent a whole year collecting good clothes and two almost-new blankets. I even got a heavy coat with a fur collar. Just like the one I had in New York when I was getting started. . . . I was a hotshot. I could whip along that deli with four platters on my arms. . . . When I moved out here and married, I got my Walter to start us up a deli, and we did real well for years. . .

> He took a hike to Vegas after his heart attack and decided to stay there. I went with him for awhile, but he got the gambling fever and didn't even know I was there. . . All our money was gone, and I came back to get a waitress job again, but I've closed two places within the last year. Got to stay in the car now. . . look at that man staring at my car. He knows I've got good stuff. He's a bum; he's got nothing. But he won't get my stuff. . . .

Crying Jags

While compulsive behavior may only be a minor affliction reflecting fears and focusing on something harmless, the constant reiteration of revenge tactics by women such as Celia (age 53, Beverly Hills, California, 1986) reveals a more serious mental disturbance. Her unresolved rage associated with victimization by an insurance agent manifests itself in sudden spurts of crying (with just as sudden stoppage) and phantasmal ideas for getting even. In-between episodes, though, she sleeps undetected in a garage behind a veterinary hospital and spends her days strolling along some of the nicest commercial streets in the country, satisfying her needs for food and "company." We meet in a park by City Hall occasionally, and most of the time she acts "normally."

> The son-of-a-bitch swore the policy was effective as of the month after it was written. When the fire broke out and ruined my house—oh, how I worked to make that a dream place—he said all I had to do was wait for a few weeks and I'd have enough to re-build. What a bastard! He hadn't turned in my check and the policy never went into effect! I tried to sue him, and the company said it was my fault for not checking back to get a receipt. . . .

> I want to get that bastard. He deserves to be spread out where the sun never sets and left to die of thirst and sunburn. Ants should eat away at his face. . . . Look what he's done to me! I had a life all planned and now I've used all my money trying to sue him and I don't have a blasted place to stay—ever! Someday. . . .

> How dare the insurance company let him get away with that. He's got a house to live in. He gets three meals a day paid for by the company. Why should I have to suffer for his incompetence? I'll make him pay! I'll make sure he suffers like I have to. I can't even get another lawyer to appeal the case. My life is ruined because of that stupid bastard. One day. . . I'll get him trapped in a yard with three vicious dobermans. Then let's see him go to work. . . He's made me so disabled that I can't even stand to fill out job applications. Why should I have to start to look for work now? I had my pension and enough to keep up my house! Now I have nothing. . . .

Prisoner of War Syndrome

Victims of domestic violence frequently characterize a particular kind of compulsive behavior which is commonly associated with male war hostages. They tell of a dysfunctional symbiotic relationship which develops between victim and victimizer, affects the entire family, and is not acted upon by service providers, mental health specialists, or the legal/judicial system—even though it could be argued that false imprisonment (a criminal offense) occurs.

Sandi (age 27, Los Angeles, California, 1986) describes how she became entrapped in this phenomenon, and sadly comments on the outcome of escape:

> For years I was a prisoner of war. Maybe that's not really right, because I could have left. But I married right after high school and had kids. Tom made me give up my friends because he didn't like them. What he didn't like was that I might have a life of my own. Anyway, I was like a prisoner in that little house. I didn't have a car, and he never gave me money for a bus or anything else. Our social life was strictly church on Sunday and he never let me out of his sight. . . .
>
> We watched TV every night. The same type of shows. All violent—like war movies, and cops shows, or the fights. Everything was someone killing or maiming. When he went off to work I got to see what life was like for other people. Not that I think everyone lives like the soaps, but all kinds of ways of living come up. And I got to see the news. He never cared what was happening outside of his job. He never voted, so I didn't get to vote. He'd take the oldest kids to school, he did the shopping, and he took the kids to the doctor. I can't ever remember getting out and doing anything for myself, or having any fun at all. I was so dependent on him that I hated him and wished he'd die. But then, what if he *did* die? I couldn't get along by myself after so many years. So I was terrified that he might die. He'd hit me for asking to go "out." He'd hit me for doing something he didn't like "in." So I loved and hated him, letting him torture me and waiting for it just to know that I was still, well, important, I guess. If he ignored me it was worse than being hurt by him. My house was my prison compound, and Tom was my captor, and I needed attention of any kind from the cruel captor. . . . I was obsessed and depressed.

But I couldn't wait to do the same things over and over again. Like I was possessed. . . . Here I am in a *shelter*. The doors are locked, bars on the windows, and someone always telling me what to do. . . or ignoring me. . . . Not much difference, is there?

Justine (age 40, Baltimore, Maryland, 1977) viewed her present situation in an introspective and retrospective manner, tied the marital syndrome to childhood and parental experiences, and noted the lack of assistance in every sector:

My dad was a career officer. We traveled from one Army post to another, and in each country we lived behind fences with barbed wire. I remember all the saluting at gates, rifles shuffled in never-ending rituals, stockades within the bigger stockade, and all of the talk about "war," whether it was a real one or one that was going to be simulated.

Mother adored him, and relied on him for everything. She was a very quiet person. She took his criticisms and strictness without being affected. But when my sisters and I questioned anything she didn't want to discuss, she became angry and spouted the same line as my father: "This is reality. Learn to live with it."

So when I married an Army man, I was used to being ordered around and while I didn't like it, I adjusted to it. He took it all too seriously, though, because he couldn't let go of his control even when we were in bed. I was ordered to get into bed. I was ordered to—well, do everything he wanted. When I objected, he treated me like I was the enemy. I learned to be submissive. My choice was to leave him, and in our family you didn't leave an Army man. My mom must have learned the same thing, and she passed it along, whether she knew it or not. . . .

The submission went too far, though. Every year his control became more pervasive, and it wasn't until I realized that I couldn't even do the laundry without fear of being verbally or physically thrashed, that I had the nerve to actually try to get help. I went to the chaplain.

He said I had to learn to understand military men. It got to be that I had to do things not just once but a couple of times. Like he made me do the dishes twice, and then the laundry, and then I found myself washing my hands twice, and I was starting to do everything twice. I couldn't seem to be satisfied unless I'd be doing things in multiples. . . I was going nuts.

Then I tried to get away one day. He caught me outside the house and brought me inside, tied me up on the floor and stood above me, feet spread apart, with gun in hand. Then he ripped off my clothes. He said I was going to stay naked forever if I didn't obey. Then suddenly he turned really red and began to blubber. He said he really loved me and he knew I loved him, and he took off his clothes and actually made love to me, caring how I felt for the first time. But I was still tied up. When we were finished, he said, "That was the best sex I ever had with anyone." And from then on, he was the best lover a woman could have—if she didn't mind having her arms tied.

I needed love so much that I let myself fall into the same trap that I'm sure my mother did. I started to remember the ropes we had in the closet and I never asked about. I remembered their bedroom. The four-poster had clamps on it. Mother said it was antique and needed support. I remembered how my father used to bellow at her in the bedroom, and how we could hear her whimper. He'd come downstairs feeling really good afterwards and ask if we [the children] would like for him to make fudge. He never made fudge at any other time. It would have been "sissy." We were all taught to be captives, to be afraid of the captor-guard, but to love him. First my father, and then my husband. We couldn't do without him because he ran every aspect of our lives. I hated him for that. But I needed him.

He may have hated us too, but he needed us in the same way, you know? Somehow the hate and love became blended, and there wasn't any way to separate them. And the only way it finally separated was when I found him tying up our daughter. She was thirteen, and I saw that same look on his face as the day he tied me up on the floor. He was excited.

I said she had a dentist's appointment, and I took the four kids, drove into town, emptied the bank account, and went to a lawyer's office. I made the lawyer blush, but I demanded a divorce that very day. I used all of my money for the lawyer, and we had to stay with relatives. I was told I would get alimony, but Ed left the country to go to another post, and by the time I found him, the relatives asked us to leave, and we had to go from one church mission to another hoping that some money would come through soon. Then the lawyer said he couldn't handle the case any longer. Legal Aid wouldn't help. My sons just disappeared one night from the mission and no agency cared. My daughter said she was going to find her father, and she left right in front of me. The police said they all left voluntarily.

Now I'm alone, living from day to day in a fog, knowing that no one is ever going to give me back a life. I just sleep in my car behind the trees over there near the edge of the shopping center parking lot, and wander around trying to find food and clothing. Sometimes I do the same things twice. I feel like I'm going to die soon. Maybe I'll die twice . . . . No one understands. A doctor at the clinic said I was depressed. Smart man. He prescribed pills I can't afford to buy. He said I needed therapy, but I think at this point I could be a therapist. I know what happened to me, and I'm not crazy.

The pills he prescribed are for serious mental patients. He probably didn't even believe anything I told him. Do you believe me?

The symbiotic relationship that develops between wife and husband as victim and victimizer is similar, then, to that which evolves between prisoners of war and their guards (and often between hostages and terrorists). The abused come to *depend* on the attention of their abusers, just as the abusers *depend* on their victims for immediate and continuing gratification. The mutual "need" is not one of love and compatibility, but one which is born dysfunctionally in physical and/or psychological intimacy, grows with time, and is intensified in relative isolation. The individuals become addicted to each other and the behaviors that perpetuate the addiction. A specific kind of intimacy is needed for this type of interaction; there is no "attachment" formed between store clerk and customer which results in the emotional base necessary for binary opposites: love/hate, torture/relief, need/disregard, attention/deprivation, or pleasure/pain. These oppositional factors are a constant feedback and response system; they are, in fact, compulsive behaviors. What begins to occur, then, is a perceptual distortion of personae. There is an anticipation of each person fulfilling an expected role; and the mutual understanding of roles leads to roleplaying wherein the individuals lose their grip on reality and begin to exist in a surrealistic realm. Many women, therefore, remain with men who "put them through hell" because they are living in "another world" sustained by this symbiotic and parasitic relationship.

The psychic impairment caused by such a dysfunctional relationship does not disappear just because the woman-victim leaves home. Its effects may follow her, affecting her ability to relate to others, to make decisions, to follow a workplace schedule, and/or to engage in social activities. Phobias often develop.

2. Phobic Behavior

Fear of People

Tina (age 38, Harper's Ferry, West Virginia, 1979) tells how she can't function among others:

I thought once I had gotten away from Billy I could get along okay. . . but sometimes I think about it being easier to get beat than tryin' to find a new place. . . I can't seem to make it now that I took off. I ain't got no relatives to take me in so I'm all alone. I—I guess I, uh, well, am scared to be with anyone new. . . .

The Y women told me to just stop feelin' sorry for myself and get along with my life. It makes me so mad. Don't they know anything about bein' on your own? I'm tryin' to live like a woman is supposed to today—like the fancy women who belong to all these women's rights groups—but I'm not like them. They all got houses and jobs. They got education and I always got the housework to do and it kept me inside and alone.

What's the matter with them? Maybe if they was forced to do things they didn't want to, well, maybe they'd get what the real world is for lots of women. The Y had speakers who all talked about how we should raise our conscious and act like men and do all the things we want. I don't know if any o' them women have anything to do with men. . . they didn't look like it. . . but they sure got ideas that don't have anything to do with real life. Especially with men like Billy. . . .

I know I got to get out there and find a new place for myself. I wish I weren't so scared that new people would do somethin' to hurt me. I guess I ain't goin' to be any modern woman like the Y women are. I need to be with some people who are all scared and aren't scared to admit that they don't do marchin' and speech-makin' and gettin' those good jobs with the other strong women. . . .

I spent the last month just going up and down the town hills raidin' the garbage cans and sleepin' in the grass near the highway. I keep thinkin' I can get the nerve to hitch, but I don't know where to go. Now I begin to shake when I just think about what's ahead. . . .

Now I look awful and I know what people are thinkin'. Maybe I should go back. Maybe I could learn how to do somethin' useful before I leave again. . . and maybe take a charm course at the high school at night. I never had any trouble meetin' people when I was younger. I'd just walk up and say 'Hi' and there was always somethin' to talk about. But I can't do that now. See how I'm shakin', and you started the talkin'. I ain't talked to anyone since a week ago when I got caught on a fence and needed help gettin' off. What's wrong with me, anyhow? I got away from Billy. . . .

Fear of Steps

Phobic behavior is often clearly related to events that have been traumatic. Pat (age 47, Baltimore, Maryland, 1973) lost the custody of her children to their father (her ex-husband) and found her way to the YWCA to ask for help in finding a job. She expressed fear of the steps and requested that someone come to the yard.

I don't mind telling you why I can't use stairways. It started when I came down the courthouse steps and suddenly became paralyzed and just stood there until I had to sit down. I stayed until it was dark and then went on my fanny to the sidewalk. . . .

It only has to be two steps. I can't bear the thought of going down. If I go up, I have to come down. I look down and get vertigo. Or something. I guess it's all psychoanalytically involved, but it's been over a year now and I'm going to have to get a job with no steps. People just think I'm crazy when I won't even go for an interview. I've been accused of not wanting a job, but honestly, it's not that. I have to have one. I'm down to my last twenty, and I've been living in the basement of the apartment house where I used to live—in the laundry room. . . .

It was a disaster, losing my kids. It wouldn't have been so bad if they were going to a good home. But they were given to their dad, and he's a terror when he's angry. He'd hit me for years, and then he started on the kids. But I didn't have any witnesses, and when I couldn't support them, he filed for their custody. The judge didn't even seem to listen to me, and every time I tried to tell him what had happened in our marriage, the judge said I couldn't.

Pat would walk for blocks to avoid steps, and knew every way into a building that didn't require her to use them. She used a window to get in and out of the basement where she had been living. People did notice her hesitating when faced with the steps, only to turn away. Often, she said, it made her cry in public. She knew that there was a relationship between losing her children in the courtroom and the onset of being "paralyzed" on the steps out of the courthouse, and she also expressed her opinion that if she could win them back she could conquer her fear of steps. Her condition was ruining her life: she could not locate employment which meant she had no money for rent or food.

3. Traditional Phenomena

Emotionally shattered women often turn to fantasizing or are prone to "unusual" experiences in which archetypic characters figure prominently. The emergence of such archetypes is exemplified in the stories I have heard for many years from pre-homeless and homeless women who have been physically and psychologically abused by husbands or lovers. Occasionally the victimizers are identified as employers, lawyers, and public officials. These actors become antagonists in tales involving supranormal visitations—both during the period in which the women are interacting with victimizers and often long after contact.

"The Old Hag"/"Hagging"

Henry Fuseli's (1781 and 1782) paintings called "The Nightmare" represent a traditional phenomenon: a terrifying bedroom intruder hovering over a flaccid and recumbent figure. The syndrome, which is perceived by the victim as occurring while awake, not a-sleep, and during which the victim feels oppressed by pressure on the chest which halts breathing, is apparently universal. This phenomenon has been labelled, for example, "the Mare" in 16th century England, *Mara* in Sweden, *augumangia* and *ukomiarik* among the Eskimo, and "the Old Hag" in Newfoundland and America.

Only one of the almost thirty women who told me about visitations which were undoubtedly "attacks by the Old Hag" had any knowledge of its traditional background. They all, however, did express similar physical and psychological symptoms. The attacks are assumed by researchers to take place during an "altered state of consciousness," in particular, that time just before sleep occurs—the hypnagogic state—and that time just as one is awakening: the hypnopompic state—and thus the intense feeling that the experience has not been a dream. In any non-waking state, archetypic figures are apt to appear as substitutes for characters who present a "real-life" threat. Unresolved problems are ripe for re-scripting in the dreamstate and in altered states of consciousness, and the homeless woman is particularly effected by lack of closure regarding a victimizer. In cases in which women are considering leaving home or have become homeless because of domestic abuse, the victimizer has betrayed the most intimate of relationships. It is often vividly apparent that there is a direct correlation between sexual intimacy and the "Old Hag" apparitional attack. The "hagging" related by Adriana (age 23, Los Angeles, California, 1986) exemplifies many which are rife with sexual symbolism:

> Well, I make up my mind not to go back with my husband. I not to take any pain anymore. I tell you again about why, but I feel some strange about talking into your machine, so maybe I not tell it the same, and you'll tell me if I do not. I not ever forget what happened. But I look at the machine and know I not talking to you like before! I say I decide not to see him again. I feel that God has told me. No, not to tell me but to give me a sign maybe. . . .

> Last month I am in the hospital again and the social worker is trying to get me to call the shelter because Raoul has beaten me too much, and this time cut me with his

switchblade. I don't want to leave him, since I am illegal and will be deported if I have no Raoul. So I go back and I tell him that if he does not go to the counseling, I am to leave. He promises never to touch me again, and for maybe a week he is nice and not hurt me in bed, and then he gets drunk and cuts me again. I let my friend take me to the police, and I sign the paper. He calls me at my friend's and swears that he is going to AA and to counseling, and maybe I'll not go to court. I say okay, because I just find out I'm pregnant, and the baby must have the father....

I lie in bed at my friend's, and I'm thinking about this baby, and thinking that maybe it shouldn't be with a man like Raoul. Then God gives me the sign. He makes Raoul come flying like a black cloud into the window, which I can see is full of sun. Raoul is changing shape, like the clouds full of rain, and he is growing. Larger than before he is growing, and as he changes the shape he is getting bigger until the big black cloud is over me, rumbling like the thunder. Then the rain falls on me, but is Raoul lying on me, and he is *so* heavy that I no can breathe. I am dying from not getting breath. I see his big switchblade moving in the cloud. It is Raoul and the cloud all in one. The blade is coming at me and I no can move. I try to call for my friend, and no sound comes out for I no can breathe. God must then tell Raoul to leave me alone for I then can breathe and the cloud is going out the window. But I see it is now smoke from the burning trash outside, and I know that I must get up and close the window. But I am so weak from being afraid that I can barely move, and for all day I pray. I know that I not to have this baby with Raoul. I go back to mother and sisters in Argentina. Safer.

While sexual *symbolism* is typified in Adriana's story, Amy (age 37, Lancaster, Pennsylvania, 1978) expresses a more explicit experience, another in which the victim experiences paralysis during the attack:

I just lay down on the sofa to catch relief from the kids. It was drizzling out, but I had the window open, and I was staring at the drops dripping down the sill onto the wallpaper. I was thinking about closing the window when the sun suddenly filled the sky and Frank was walking right in through the window. I know that sounds crazy, but this great big man just came in, which is kind of funny anyway since Frank is a little guy, and he stood on the edge of the sofa. He towered over me and leered at me just the way he always did when he wanted sex. I knew if I didn't give him exactly what he wanted, I'd get my face punched, so I just lay there watching him. I mean, I couldn't have moved if I'd wanted to because I felt almost paralyzed. . . .

He threw himself on me and crushed me into the sofa. I could feel him pushing down too hard and his bullets belt buckle was jabbing me. He kept pushing up and down on me like I was being stabbed with the buckle each time. I felt like all the air was being pushed out of my lungs and I tried to pull away but couldn't move at all. I was so tired that I just gave up and began to cry. But I wasn't crying. I wasn't moving at all or breathing for a minute, and then he drifted off me like a leaf and blew right out the window, getting smaller and smaller until I was looking at a raindrop dripping down the wallpaper. . . .

It was the most scary thing that ever happened to me, and I can't understand any of it. I don't think I was asleep. I was wide awake. I know one thing for sure. I'm cured of Frank forever.

The use of a weapon by the "hagging" abuser has both symbolic and realistic significance. The weapon almost always described has been of phallic shape: knife, gun, broom handle, baseball bat, or hammer. Further, it is usually "jabbed" or "thrust" (often repeatedly) into the woman's abdominal or chest region, rendering her breathless or exhausted. The actual experiences of abuse by husband or lover have involved those same weapons.

Another unusual feature which is often mentioned by victims is the larger-than-life size of the attacker. While it might not seem peculiar that an apparition would appear larger than an ordinary person, the women have been impressed by the disparate size between the husband/lover (and in two documented cases, a lawyer and an employer) and the "hagging" figure. In the case of a woman physically and/or psychologically abused by a husband/lover, one must consider the undue amount of control that such an abuser employs in her daily life and in the supranormal experience. The smaller/real-life man exercised physical and emotional control over his wife, but she had always managed to manipulate the situation by being able to *move*. None of the victims of the supranormal assault could move, indicating a *greater* degree of vulnerability and possible death. Fear preceded the attack, fear was ever-present in the victim's mind, and fear was magnified during the apparitional appearance. Fear remained a factor long after the attack, influencing the victim's sleep pattern and ability to cope with ordinary activities. These disablements are often expressed by homeless women.

Eve (age 28, Los Angeles, California, 1986) reveals the effects of an extremely fearful experience.

> I had to spend two months in the locked ward last year. I had this awful dream twice in a row, and I told the doctor that it wasn't no dream, but he put me away anyway. . . .

> I know that Harvey came into my room in the hospital and tried to kill me, but the doctor said he was in jail at the time. I *know* that I was sort of drowsy on medication from surgery, but I was awake enough to be watching a TV show and I could tell the doctor what it was about. He says I was nuts because I said that Harvey came at me with his big old knife and lay down on me in the bed and put the knife right up to my throat and pressed the handle so tight against my vocal cords that I couldn't scream for help. I lay there and sweated and choked and looked into his eyes. He was all

blurry, and I guess that was my medication, but he was there and I felt every hair on my body being touched.

When I told the nurse, she told the doctor, and he said I was crazy and they put me away. I know what happened, and it scares me even today. If that hadn't happened, though, I probably would be dead, but I never went back. I been on my own ever since, and as scared as I am now being alone all the time and not knowing where I'll sleep tomorrow, I was more scared then.

It is not unusual for the person who describes a numinous (or supranormal) encounter to be thought of and labelled as mentally ill. It is undoubtedly a major factor in the dearth of such taletellings. Victims of domestic abuse have an added burden: few people believe that any woman in her right mind would stay with a man who beats her. Consequently, the victim keeps "secret" many of the stories which she would like to share with others, only reconstructing the events to herself: idionarrating.

Will-o'-the-Wisps (and Jack-O-Lanterns)

"Haggings" are not the only supranatural experiences recounted by homeless women. Will-o'-the-Wisps are traditional "figures" associated with sightings of a luminescent ball or bobbing lights near swamps and bogs. It is common in tradition to hear of Will-o'-the-Wisps and Jack-O-Lanterns (a similar light-related creature) in rural areas or in cemeteries, but occasionally the blinking lights are seen in urban settings. While individuals reporting these lights are not usually considered to be "mentally ill," the *homeless woman* is likely to be so identified. Her state of mind is pre-determined by her marginal status, as Henrietta (age 64, St. Michaels, Maryland, 1978) notes:

I was just doing what I always do—walking along the road near the river [which is in-town]. I thought my eyes were playing tricks on me, but I kept blinking and the little lights were really there. . . They sort of, uh, um,—well—blipped and bumped from the edge of the road to the water and back again. Like they were beckoning to me to follow them. Well, I guess I was, oh, hypnotized, maybe, by the dipping and back and forth movement, and I—my feet—just went toward the lights. I didn't realize that they, um, danced like, over the water until I was almost falling into the river. I'd walked right down the slope without really watching where I was going. . . . I could have been killed. . . .

Well, you can guess what happened when I went into the grocery and told the clerk that I'd just seen a willywisp. He looked at me as if I were absolutely nuts, and that's silly 'cause we all know folks have been telling stories about them since frogs was tadpoles. Is that right? Funny, I can't remember now if that's what frogs come from! Well, he must a told some others, 'cause since then I was branded as nuts. Now if Mrs. Rich-as-you-come had said she saw a willywisp, there'd be a whole bunch of reporters following her around for more information! I'm just a newcomer who meanders around town and stays in her van a lot, and I'm a pretty good set-up for being nuts. . . .

Ghosts

Ghosts who return from the dead are also responsible, according to a few victims of homelessness, for their situation. Rena (age 63, Cockeysville, Maryland, 1977) described her experience with the ghost of the previous owner of the house in which she lived with her husband:

I know this sounds absolutely insane, but we lived in this house where the man died and keeps coming back to get revenge on whatever woman is living there. My husband and I were happy until we moved there. . . . we never had any trouble. But soon after we moved in, we knew there was something funny going on. Lights and noises and all the stuff you see in stupid movies. My husband would be a-sleep, and suddenly he would wake up and begin hitting me. He would say later that it wasn't him at all, but some man who was all lit up that took over his body. Well, you know what I called that! It got worse. A neighbor started telling me about the man who used to live there and how much he hated women because his wife had left him. I didn't believe it at first, but my husband got so bad that I couldn't stay there anymore....

Who would believe me? I tried to explain, but everyone thought I was bananas. My minister told me to stop talking about ghosts. My lady friends said I needed a shrink. But my husband changed. All the time he was thinking about this man, and he got to hating women too. I think that this ghost just took over his mind and body. I asked for alimony, but he went bankrupt to make sure I couldn't get any money. I'm lucky just to have gotten the car, and I'm living in it and working part-time in a department store. You know that's not enough to live on. I don't see any real future for me....

4. UFOs and Alien Visitors

Sightings of unexplained lights are not restricted to Will-o'-the-Wisps and Jack-O-Lanterns; since the 1950s there has been a plethora of UFO sightings, and almost all viewers note lights as part of the phenomenon. While a strong imagination and sobriety are usually suspected after a UFO sighting, there is not really a suggestion that seeing traveling lights in the sky indicates failing mental health. However, when the close encounter of the first kind (a sighting) becomes a close encounter of the third kind (meeting aliens) and especially of the fourth kind (being in physical contact with the extraterrestrial), one's mental health is definitely a consideration. There is, perhaps, a rational explanation for a *homeless woman* to insist that she has been the target for exposure and/or the object of examination. Her coping mechanism in dealing with marginality—physical and/or social isolation—may be to substitute communication with interplanetary beings for sociability with humans. Gretchen (age 32) was raised in Germany, married a serviceman, and moved to San Francisco when she was nineteen. At twenty-six she had three children, a divorce, and was moving constantly to avoid her in-laws who threatened to take the children away from her. They finally succeeded (by a court order, which she insists was "fixed") and Gretchen began to roam. It was shortly after she had settled in Santa Maria that she says she met interplanetary travelers. When I met her in 1983, she was explaining that these beings had followed her to Los Angeles and were repeatedly examining her.

> I have just had to adjust to the medical examinations. I certainly tried to escape from these creatures. I moved around, but they followed me. I guess they use telepathy to find me, because they always communicate with me through the mind. No real words are spoken, except by me, and I sometimes don't do that anymore. I can think a conversation and they always answer that way. . . .
>
> I don't know why they are so interested in my physical being, but several times I have been transported by a white beam and been probed by some kind of X-Rays. Then I sort of feel their limbs poking me, especially in the breast and pelvic regions. One creature asked me all about how we create new people, and then a couple of them had long talks with me about sexual acts.
>
> I was told that some of them now live on earth as people, and that the beam can find me, take me to the ship, and then to their planet. It's not a threat, really. I get the feeling now that they want to be friends with me, and that I can talk to them about anything. I do.
>
> I don't have anyone else to be friends with, so I'm happy to have someone—anyone—who cares about me. Maybe the other planet will be better.

Gretchen's loss of her family and friends hypothetically contributed to a propensity to form alternative personal attachments, despite her insistence that she tried to avoid contact with these beings. The aliens listen to her and perpetrate no harm. They perform intimately with her, both cognitively and physically. Her identity as "a woman" is validated; she is important "as is." The extraterrestrials provide understanding and are a source of fellowship. That special bonding is insidiously affecting Gretchen's belief in travel to and life on another planet.

Phillipa (age 35, Santa Monica, California, 1986) is already "committed" to an alien who will eventually become her husband. Her stories lead one to believe that she is, indeed, mentally ill; but no one has "listened" to her constant pleas for legal assistance in regaining a job from which she was fired by an employer who tried (unsuccessfully) to prove that missing funds were her fault, she has been rejected by every appropriate social service agency, her only child was killed in a hit-and-run incident by a drunk driver with multiple arrests, and she has no money to continue her fight for forest preservation activities. The friends she had have moved or no longer wish to hear of her misfortunes. Accustomed to rejection and disappointment, she has simply devised a tool to cope with life as it exists for her. If she had alternatives to Tor and Hyperion for problem-solving, she would probably find some peace on earth.

> I won't be here long enough for you to do anything for me, but thank you for trying to help. I will be going to Hyperion as soon as Tor receives permission to have me transformed into Hyperion form and taken aboard one of their spacecrafts. I'm supposed to be ready at any minute. It won't hurt, of course. I'll just stand in the beam of light, feel real good, and drift up the beam in their form. Then I'll have a really good life on Hyperion with Tor. . . .

> Do you know they can't have killings? It just can't happen. Something stops anything that is going to harm someone. And they don't have any diseases or freaky weather or planetary threats, either. They solved what we're all still pretending we're working on. . . .

> Everyone treats everyone else the way they should. They don't need politicians because there just aren't any problems

with what we call government. Everyone obeys the laws of nature and what is best for everyone's survival. . . .

They have a system of equal voice, and each voice has good ideas. They all listen. . . .

5. Near-Death Experiences

The "beam of light" is also significant in the stories told by women who report a near-death experience (NDE). Ann (age 39, Washington, D.C., 1978) was living in a major mall complex in Virginia when I found myself sitting beside her while my companion continued shopping. She began the conversation by asking for a cigarette. I said I did not smoke. She then told me that she was not supposed to smoke because she had recently been released from the hospital. After much small-talk about hospitals, she revealed that she had been in a "mental unit"; her husband had had her put there to "get her out of the way." She had walked out with a visitor and had been living in the mall area for several months. She may sound paranoid, but it would be easy enough for someone to check the facts of the rape, hospitalization, and bank signatures.

I was recovering from being raped by the men my husband hired. He wanted a divorce and I wouldn't give him one. Not because I loved him or my religion is against it, but because he would get all of my stocks and bonds. So when I heard one of the men say his name by accident while they were taking turns torturing me, I knew he hired them. So I went to a girlfriend's house afterwards, and she called the police and then she took me to an emergency hospital. . . .

I guess I went into shock. The doctors said I had a peculiar reaction to a shot. Anyway, I remember exactly what happened. I was resting in the bed in the recovery room, and I saw this little bit of white light grow into a long ray that extended from my bed to and beyond the window. I was lifted off the bed and moved into the light, and as I looked back I could see the bed and me on it. I just kept moving up the ray and out of the window—which was closed—and I was like on an escalator going skywards. I felt very good. All the pain was gone, and my mind was filled with thoughts of forgiveness. You see, I was really angry while I was in the emergency room being treated. Then I got to a certain spot where the light became a big glow, and I was put down on, well, a cloud, I guess. Then I heard voices saying I wasn't ready yet, and I had to go back. I didn't know what that meant, but somehow I was back on the ray and going back down the shaft to the hospital room. I could see it below me as I approached it, and I could see me on the bed when I was back in the room. I opened my eyes and a nurse said I was okay, but there was all the pain again, and I was still angry. I know that I died and came back to life. . . .

No one believed me, and my husband got a couple of psychiatrists to say that I was nuts, and suddenly I found myself in the mental unit of [a hospital] and I couldn't get out. I did one night, and the next morning I went to my bank and then to my accountant, and everything I owned was signed over to my husband. It looked like my signature, but I know I never signed anything. So here I am, hoping that no one recognizes me. This is a wig, and my makeup is all different. I can't stay here forever, but I'm afraid to contact any of my friends. Maybe they will tell my husband where I am and I'll be back in the nuthouse. No one is ever going to believe me.

I wish I had stayed dead.

6. Religious Experiences

The NDE is often noted by informants to be associated with a religious experience. Sarah (age 59, Boothbay, Maine, 1976) was living in a decrepit motor home (which doubled as her sales wagon) when I stopped to buy rolls from her during a period of homelessness. I was counting-out my pennies when she asked me if I "needed the rolls free." Embarrassed yet always ready to tell my story to get one, I told her of my predicament. She invited me into her old vehicle for coffee. I was not surprised to hear that "the locals think me balmy" and that she could articulate clearly if she wanted to. I do not know how many people saw her icon-filled motor home, but it would only take one in a small community to pass the word that a crazy, religious fanatic lived among them. There was not one space left on a wall or table for another religious item.

I been living in this bus for a few years now, ever since my Henry burned down our house and took off with some little snit who thought she saw money. Huh! What a jolt she must have got. . . .

I didn't think I'd make it in the beginning. What do you do when suddenly you got nothing? The few friends I had began to pretend I didn't exist, and the offers of food and a bed disappeared. One night I got drunk and passed out down by the bridge, and I woke up with dirt in my mouth and no desire to do anything but die. I must have lay there for a whole day. I didn't have no place to go. I got hold of some clams, and they must have been bad, because I got food poisoning and I figured I was going to die. Didn't bother me.

While I was waiting to die, I felt like I got lifted up from the ground and was floating around on top of my real body. I knew I was in trouble when a figure of a lady with a halo and a long white dress started floating in front of me, beckoning me to move with her. I did. I was looking down at the river as we floated over it. I tried to get closer to her, to see who she was, but she kept just that far from me. It seemed a long time before we stopped, and it was on top of a church in Wiscasset. We just sat on the roof. Then I could see that she was Mary, and while I was staring at her, she pointed down to a car that was parked off in the bushes. Then she disappeared, and I just floated back to where I had been.

The next thing I knew, I was throwing up and a guy in a white suit said "thank God, she's going to be all right." He kept saying I had been dead to the people standing around, and I guess that I knew I had been dead and been visited by Mary and brought back to life by her. I said I was fine, they all left finally, and I don't know how long it took—probably a day—to get to Wiscasset on my shaky feet and don't you know, there was this motor home just where Mary showed me. I couldn't believe it, but I been thanking her and talking with Mary every day now. I don't understand it, really, but I know that I was dead and that a religious miracle happened.

Sarah said she was an atheist before that experience—which probably explains her surprise at a visitation by Mary (in particular). What Sarah did find was "someone" to communicate with when she needed it most. The selection of Mary may be associated with a questioning of her lack of belief; her religiosity may have been a matter of concern which had been preying on her mind. Sarah made it very plain to me that she did not invite people into her motor home, but that she felt there was something special about me. She said that she talked only to Mary, and that she did so almost constantly. I saw her several times before she moved on to another location, and I never heard her converse with anyone else beyond quoting a sales price for her small supply of breads. I asked about her in the pharmacy, and the only response I received was that she was a "fruitcake who used to live down past the old schoolhouse."

Norma (age 63, Los Angeles, California 1988) insists that angels appeared to save her from a police officer who was (apparently) just about to take her to jail:

I just don't have the money to buy tags for my car. I always back up into a parking space against a wall or something so that my license plate doesn't show. . . .

I knew I was in trouble when the police car followed me from the main road into a one-laner. No one ever goes down that road except the few people who live there and me. I park down the road about two miles and no one knows I'm living there....

He followed me for about a mile and then turned on his lights. I nearly panicked. I had to pull over at the nearest point, and my heart was racing and I thought I was going to faint. He wanted to see my registration and license and none of mine are up to date. . .so I started to tell him about what had happened to me and he was as stone-cold faced as anyone can be. He went back to his car and was using the radio. Probably to see if the car was stolen. Then he came back and said my car had to be taken in. I had a few tickets that I couldn't afford to pay. . . and the car payments were overdue. I began to faint. There was a funny sound. Like, ahh, maybe faraway horns. Then I heard little fluttering noises, and then they got louder. I looked over my shoulder and there they were. Angels. Cherubs? I don't know except that they were suddenly all around me and sort of putting up a protective shield. The cop began to go further away, umm, like being pushed away by all the fluttering angels around me. He got pushed all the way to his car. . . I just sat there feeling kind of lightheaded and saw his car pull out and go past me. He just went on up the road....

I know God sent the angels to save me. I know you're going to say that's crazy. I don't care. But there's no other explanation for him leaving me alone like that....

While the religious aspect has been mentioned by many homeless women as their source of inspiration to continue, it has also been subject for source of pain and actual injury. Clare (age 33, Los Angeles, California, 1985) blames her husband's particular religious practices for her physical abuse; she says he "pinned a doll" which directly caused her abdominal pain and broken ribs.

That man, he's into voodoo, and he can hurt me any time he wants to. I found the doll all pinned after he done it once and I didn't know why I was hurting. When I told him I'd tell the cops, he just laughed. He was right. They told me they couldn't arrest anyone for playing with a doll. He'd have to touch me first. Well, he never touches me; he just pins that old doll, and I know when he does, 'cause I have to go to the hospital. Each time there's something broken, so you tell me how it happens. I don't live with him anymore. I sleep on a bench at the beach. So I can't be told that I know when it will happen. . . .

I tried to get a Catholic priest to stop all the voodoo stuff, but he said he couldn't. But he couldn't explain why bones were broken.

He tried to tell me that voodoo isn't a religion, but he doesn't know anything about it at all. Voodoo is a religion, and if you believe, then it's just as strong as any other one. I never believed before; now I do. There's real power there. Maybe more than other religions.

This is not an isolated case of claimed voodoo-induced injury. It is of particular interest when the victim desires to file a complaint against an abuser with the office of the district attorney or city attorney. Psychological damage is not a basis for filing charges; physical injury is necessary. Pictures are usually required, even if police officers have seen bruises. In addition, it must be proven that an abuser has actually touched the victim's body—whether it be by hand or object. While it is sometimes possible to prove that injury was (for example) deliberately caused by a rope stretched across the top of a stairway (resulting in the victim's fall), I do not know of any case in which the prosecution won on the grounds of physical injury caused by voodoo. While Clare found no sympathetic ears within the court system, she did find camaraderie within a community of believers, and that is where she tells her stories of voodoo-induced injuries. She has explained to me that there are several women who have tried to find the answer to blocking the influence of the pinned doll. They find solace in studying various religious practices and incorporating this knowledge into their belief system. This provides new experiences to share—and isolation is replaced with sociability.

The bright light that often is a prelude to or part of a supranormal encounter such as a hagging; a near-death experience; the sighting of a UFO, Will-o'-the-Wisp, or a ghostly figure; or a religious experience seems to be significant. In all cases there is a connection between luminosity and numinosity. What is seen and what is unknown appear to conjoin to raise questions concerning hallucinatory experiences—or altered states of consciousness—and physical, psychological, cultural, religious, and universal factors. *Homo sapiens* expresses awe or fear of and reverence for fire and light. In Christian belief, Christ is the light of the world, and fire is an important symbol—from the Burning Bush to the spiritual warmth generated for joy, peace, and purification. Halos surround religious figures. The menorah of the Jewish religion is a seven-branched candelabrum as used in the Temple in Jerusalem. The bright "white (or blue) beam" which is part of an NDE usually has a religious significance. The flames of Hell house Satan. Light and fire are associated with witches and sorcery. The glow that accompanies Will-o'-the-Wisps, Jack-O-Lanterns, and imps are similar to the flickering and darting lights of UFOs. Universally, people utilize flames to entice or dispel spirits from the Upper and Lower Worlds. Candlelight and/or (sometimes symbolic) flame is common during many traditional ceremonies, from rites of passage in primitive societies to urban organizational celebrations. One's state of mind is not necessarily unbalanced, therefore, when reporting flickering or steady bright lights; it appears that we are cross-culturally socialized to relate some such lights to numinous occurrences.

What have we learned from hearing about the various beliefs and behaviors which are so often labelled "mental illness"? For one thing, we can differentiate between true mental illness and what can be called "psychic impairment." I have borrowed that term from a landmark 1974 case in which attorneys for the plaintiffs—residents of a West Virginia coal mining town which disappeared in a flood caused by the negligence of dam operators—argued that "mental illness" has an invalid connotation for varying degrees of psychiatric damage which can result from trauma and loss. In that particular case, psychic impairment included psychiatric damage (disturbances long after the flood) and the loss of communality, a condition heretofore unrecognized by law as grounds for recovery. I am analogizing the loss of personal and social relationships—communality—by Buffalo creek residents with the loss of such relationships by victims of homelessness. Just as the residents of Buffalo Creek suffered a variety of disturbances eighteen months after the flood which destroyed their closely-knit community, women (and children) who have lost any unit depended upon for emotional sustenance (family, close friends, church members, neighborhoods) suffer a variety of disturbances, one of which is mental distress distinguishable from what we consider to be the effects of "normal" stress. By separating the states of mind and particular behaviors which are "mental illness" and "psychic impairment," appropriate assistance can be determined and generated.

There has been a long-standing discussion among professionals in various fields regarding "post-traumatic stress syndrome." There is a consensus of thought which acknowledges the existence of physical and mental distress after particularly offensive or violent acts (the "severe traumas" which quite obviously interfere with the quality and structure of life [e.g., incest, witnessing the murder of parents or children, and war-related torture]), but not after the differentiated "less harmful" events of daily life, which would include domestic strife, being forced to relocate to keep one's job, or being denied legal assistance. There is little consensus as to what constitutes the division line. At what point, for instance, does rape pass from a "simple domestic squabble" to a "severe traumatic event," or, when does being forced to relocate one's employment pass from "another of life's injustices" to a "traumatic end to a career"? And when do "post" trauma symptoms begin—immediately after the event or as a "delayed" reaction? The researcher's answers to these questions can affect how a homeless woman is evaluated. Rarely is the victim asked to offer self-evaluation. Nor—and more importantly—is she asked to propose solutions to the problems which she can outline as causing her situation. Personal experience narratives, however, are tools for diagnosis and intervention, and it is reasonable to expect that professionals should use any tool that effectuates aid to clients as well as to the larger society.

In the last chapter, I have prepared an overview of the points made in chapters 1 through 5, and with further stories by homeless women, direct your attention to what can be accomplished in the way of prevention and remedy. In response to a call to service by homeless women, a churchwomen's movement is proposed to tackle the problems which have not been resolved by "the women's movement."

Chapter Six

The Light: A Churchwomen's Movement

Given that most homeless women do not participate in social communication which evokes brainstorming and the opportunity for subsequent problem-solving, the eradication of homelessness becomes a task for other women and organizations. One looks immediately to the causes and conferences of feminist activists. International conferences (e.g., the 1976 United Nations Habitat Conference, which generated the 1987 Global Forum [in Nairobi] and the 1988 Habitat International Coalition [in New Delhi]) have focused on coalition-building in defense of the rights of the poor, homeless and inadequately housed, including the recent establishment of the worldwide, regionally-based Women and Shelter Network. In North America, Canadian women have networked and created grassroots housing and economic opportunities more effectively than have their United States counterparts, despite individual and small-group efforts which are suffering from fluctuating funding, isolation, and staff turnover, and therefore experience varied degrees of success. The "women's movement" in the United States has not addressed homelessness with the same interest and aggressiveness as other, preferred issues; feminists discuss leaving relationships in which there is domestic abuse, shelters for immediate lodging, and the need for affordable housing without really focusing on the fact that these women are *homeless*. The (non-

173

feminist) national coalitions which concentrate on the care of the homeless have taken little notice of the growing, hidden (not street-scene) population of lone, mainly over-forty borderline and home-less women all across the country. At the four-day, 1987 Governor's Conference in California, I was the only speaker/workshop leader to discuss homelessness (in general and specifically as a problem correlated with domestic abuse). I do not know if further discussion was invited in 1988 or 1989, but the 1990 Governor's Conference program has reference to women currently homeless *only* in relation to rape survival and assumably as part of the "homeless youth and AIDS" population. The only correlation between domestic violence and *possible* homelessness concerns gays and lesbians.

I suggest that pre-homeless and homeless women need new ad-vocates, and the most logical advocates are the *mainstream* women of America. While it is often touted that mainstream women are in-volved in "the women's movement," many women who consider themselves "mainstream" do not identify or have any association with NOW or the National Coalition Against Domestic Violence, the two major organizations dedicated to (particular aspects of) women's rights. Since "the women's movement" has other priorities to pursue, there seems to be no alternative but to create a *new* national women's organization with local "chapters" to center on the millions of females who are at risk of becoming homeless—and the untold number who are already living in vehicles, malls, terminals, abandoned buildings, garages, and so on.

Just who are the "mainstream" women of America and what are their concerns? And how *can* mainstream women manage the or-ganizing, resourcing, and webworking necessary to meet the chal-lenge of eliminating—or at the very least, alleviating—homeless-ness? By my definition, mainstream women attend to home, work, children, community needs, and integrate spirituality into their daily lives. They feel deeply about social issues but rarely have the opportunity to do more than sign a petition, vote, commit a modicum of hours to volunteerism, and donate money or tangibles. They are the real "backbone" of America, for they are diversified in their interests and participation; they are not so bound to one aspect of life that all others are omitted. Their commonality emerges in the way they feel about scripture: they believe that to live a joyful and meaningful life constitutes practicing what their biblical role models present as guidelines for attitude and action. Those guidelines represent social responsibility.

I am basing my proposal, a new *churchwomen's movement*, on the potentiality of the mainstream woman and her house of worship. Religious women across the United States often meet weekly and bring canned food and clothing for the needy. But their commitment and abilities are constrained by small numbers, inadequate information, and separatism; the usual networking is between local churches and temples of similar philosophy and out-of-community "sister" churches. Canned food and used clothes are often stockpiled until an outlet is located; and more often than not it is a "Skid Row" area which receives the bulk of goods since missions and downtown churches can more easily distribute donations: highly-visible homeless come forth to ask for assistance. It is the rare uptown church or temple whose members act together in "hands-on" service by preparing and serving meals and actually fitting clothes to homeless people in their own community—even though such a population may be noted. Consequently, leadership on the local level is needed to do two things: create the climate for direct services and bring isolated, committed congregations together for an organized workforce. When the local network has become a functioning unit which can address connected neighborhood needs on its own ground, then it is time for an expansion of services beyond the community—and in this era of computerized telecommunications, that is not as difficult as it may seem. But it is within each community that particular problems are identified and solutions can be tested; the servant-leader model can be utilized to address needs in a pragmatic manner.

This is not a new concept, for it is within the Judeo-Christian tradition that those who are "able" aid those less fortunate in the community. While we tend to think in terms of personal assistance for individuals-in-need and support of employment opportunities for community survival, what inevitably emerges is attendance to thoughtful land and property management. Stewardship becomes a technique not just for serving the human condition, but for controlling the way in which we assess and use the land on which we live and the buildings which we construct. It is not possible to value the [wo]man and not value the issues which encompass how that person lives, works, and plays. Throughout history, committed people have understood the connection between human dignity and land use. Settlements have been intentionally formed just to assure that the land and its economic value benefit the quality of human life. What is going to be discussed further in this chapter is not "communal" (as in commune) development as a partial solution to unemployment, lack of suitable housing, the loss of aesthetic and environmentally-conscious urban "open spaces," and unsound community spirit, but a relatively new concept and practice which calls for a democratically-run, not-for-profit organizational effort based on the premise that community members live and thrive on the land which the organization—a *community land trust*—owns and leases in perpetuity to home owners or renters. This major benefit to those who are the most disadvantaged in society will be examined in the context of how the average religious woman can participate in improving her own community. Other projects will also be explored.

Within the personal experience narratives of homeless women, we have heard complaints regarding private and public sector individuals and systems. Let us now focus on the *solutions* they offer to the omissions, misrepresentations, and mismanagements which lead directly to victimization and homelessness. In each story there is a message or a plan which can be utilized to promote awareness, empowerment, self-sufficiency, community building, and justice. There is an implicit (if not explicit) call to service to Christian women, although that is not meant to exclude the commitment and deeds of the non-Christian female who is just as eager to serve. (As an example of the power of organized religious women, one only has to take notice of the two major groups which provide more coordinated, caring services than all of the public sector agencies combined: the Catholic Charities and the Jewish Family Services.) For the purpose of constructing a viable churchwomen's movement,

I am going to work "from the ground up": from the neighborhood to the nation, so to speak. In this manner, all women can relate to the role they can play in a large movement with a variety of strategies and projects.

1. From the Shadows of the Physical Environment

"I didn't have to be homeless," said Dolores (age 44, Baltimore, Maryland, 1979). "All I needed was a chance to get a job. But after five weeks on the street, I looked a mess. I was embarrassed to go on an interview. Now I'm hopeless."

Hopelessness comes very quickly after losing one's source of stability: shelter, food, bath, and appropriate clothing. Even the immediately-formerly-employed experience that surge of fear and powerlessness when they realize that they no longer can compete with those who have the luxury of safety, privacy, and cleanliness. How can this be remedied?

I tried the missions right after I landed in town. My God, what horrors! If the bedbugs didn't get you, the thieves did. I was afraid to get anywhere near those slovenly women, but there wasn't any choice. The places were jammed with people who looked like they'd been on the streets for months and had stopped caring. . . . I got into a shelter for battered women in Indianapolis. For a few weeks I thought I'd have a chance to recuperate and get back on my feet with a new job and an apartment. But we weren't allowed to stay long enough to make a difference. . . not that it mattered. I didn't have a minute of quiet to think. It wasn't an atmosphere where anyone could plan, or sleep when you wanted to, or move around freely. And there really wasn't any help, even though they meant well. . . .

You know what's needed? A private room and a library full of books about all the ways a woman can get the aid she needs and info on school grants and someone to head you in the right direction. With plenty of time to get back into life without thinking that you got that eight-weeks limit coming up and you'll have to go to the street the same way you came in. . . . They had plenty of clothes that came in, but they were all mixed-up and not right for any of our needs. . . .

When I lived in the South, there was lots of rooms empty in those big old convents. I don't know what the church folk was planning to do with those buildings, but wouldn't they be great for. . . oh, you know, like rooming houses in the old days. And the nuns, well, they would be just great for helping us get the right frame of mind and pointing us in the right direction. They listen. And they don't make you feel like you're gonna be thrown out of their lives. [Bonnie, age 33, Los Angeles, California, 1987]

Every church sponsors study groups. One in-depth research project might be focused on local land and buildings owned by the church, their status in relation to use, and a well-written proposal to church leaders for the (at least temporary) utilization of vacant space by homeless women. In addition, the proposal should include the ways in which all women involved in the church—not just nuns—could volunteer time and expertise: an educational program leading to formal schooling which would create a career, information on and instruction for cottage industries, the establishment of a shared-housing network in the community (for example, matching seniors who cannot live alone in their homes with compatible homeless women who can provide companionship and needed chores), group support sessions in which women can share concerns and hopes, a buddy-system of resumé writing and job hunting, the coordination of donated clothing into units which could be exchanged with other churches for maximum use, and a networking among church members and known apartment owners for the accommodation of several women for an undesignated length of time—the sponsorship paid for by a specific fund accumulated from the profits of events. In the matter of fund-raising, it is the neighborhood woman who is the expert on garage sales, potluck dinners and food sales, dinner dances, raffles, gaming nights, and so on.

Speakers, especially celebrities, on interesting topics are one way to make a simple potluck dinner into a money-making project.

The Catholic Church in particular has many well-constructed buildings that are not used to capacity in addition to a surplus of untouched or under-utilized land. The women of each parish could offer to prepare rooms (where available) for occupancy and be responsible for their upkeep (not in the sense of housekeeping, but rather as monitors for cleanliness, safety, and preservation), as well as network with men in the community who could construct (temporary, if necessary) buildings of any size which could be socially beneficial. Retreat buildings could be studied for any number of rooms which would be appropriate as temporary or semi-permanent lodging with the exchange of duties as payment until jobs are located and salaries permit a move into an apartment. The roles of local religious women, then, in arranging for different kinds of housing for homeless women would range from researchers to educators to networkers to fund-raisers to cooks and painters.

The very basis for life—sustenance—seems to cause the most complex problems for community outreach, even though food is the easiest commodity to provide. We forget that homeless people may not have the proper utensils for opening, cooking, and eating canned foodstuffs. Health department codes and sanitation laws too often rule out the distribution of unsalable edibles from restaurants and grocery stores. High-visibility homeless will more often appear for "line-ups" than those who remain in a "hidden" or non-mobile lifestyle. Gatherings of visibly-homeless may understandably disturb neighborhood residents, especially when the "line-ups" occur in parks or where children play. What can the churchwoman do? Individual churches can be targeted as central points for direct fresh-food preparation and service, the advertisement of such free buffets provided by vouchers given to the known needy and by word-of-mouth to neighborhood women who are seen often in an area. This need not be an affront to dignity; a church buffet is attended by all members of a community and does not put the least advantaged in the limelight. If *all* churches in a community are responsible for the commitment *of a certain amount and type of food on a continuing basis*, the organization of feeding the poor becomes not a hit-and-miss affair, but rather like a smoothly-run "catering service." All it takes is networking among the church memberships to decide where the food will be most useful and how the division of duties will be arranged. In some areas, the boxing and distributing of nutritious and tasty food may be propitious—as in the hills or according to weather restrictions. Initial cooperative ventures open doors to more complicated networking among the churches of one large community and several communities which may be separated by distance as well as ethnic, cultural, and social ties.

2. From the Shadows of the Economic Structure

While many women want traditional office/store jobs, just as many would rather engage in a cottage industry. But most women do not even recognize that they have the ability to operate such a private, home-based business. Too often a marketable skill—usually traditional handcrafts or food preparation—is assumed to be something done for self-pleasure, need, or donation. To discover that there is monetary value in a skill learned from a family member or close friend and long-practiced is often a shock, as it was to Maggie (age 47, Newcastle, Maine, 1976):

> Gee, if I'd known that anyone would buy my rush and cattail baskets, I'd have been in business long before I took some to the Sunday flea market. I thought I might get a few dollars for food, but I didn't expect that people would snap them up and ask for more!
>
> It's funny, you know? I've lived near the marshes since I was a baby, and my mother and her mother always made our chair seats and sofa bottoms from the rushes. When I was little, I was sent out to bring back an armful to repair what daddy always broke when he sat down too hard, and I watched how my mother and sisters cleaned, cut, shaped, and then wove the rushes into tight squares. We'd get bored with the plain patterns, so we'd create our own, trying to use

the shades of natural grass and blending them with some darker reeds and whatever else grew in the freshwater and nearby saltwater marshes. Sometimes there was fierce competition to see whose was more attractive. That was usually in the winter when we had nothing to do except stay in the house....

When I was old enough, I was just told to make a new chair bottom the way some people are told to go bake a pie. Now I can do that too, but I somehow knew that if I could bake a really terrific pie, it would be something I could sell. I never thought of the rushes as anything but something needed. Certainly not something that anyone outside of the family would ask for—or want to buy when I made them into baskets or bottoms ready to be tacked onto chairs.

Now I only have this little place to stay, and it isn't mine, so I may be kicked out at any time, but I have this sudden *business*! I can see that by next year I just may be able to rent a place for myself and make a go of this permanently.

Similarly, Hilda (age 41, Lancaster, Pennsylvania, 1979) had no idea that her family recipe for fruit and vegetable breads was the basis for a business:

Since I was a little kid I watched and helped my grandmother and then my mother make dessert-like breads from the produce we picked. It was something economical for us; it didn't cost much and they were so tasty that no one really minded that we didn't have too much else to eat that we had to buy. The breads went well with eggs from our neighbor's chickens and the always-on-the-stove soup made from whatever we could scare up....

When I first got noticed was at a church bazaar last year. I had to go just to pile up some food for myself since I was down to my last dollar and I couldn't get a lawyer to get any money from my husband—who was living in our home while I was living in my car. So I made a loaf of spiced apple and pear bread and one of carrot and potato—thanks to a woman in the church kitchen—and took those into the church hall so I didn't have to look like a vagrant. No one saw that I had lots of little plastic bags and tin foil in my pockets to take away much more than I came in with. Did you know that a lot of women are living that way? I've noticed other women actually going from one church affair to another just to stock up on food, and in our area you can live pretty well that way if no one spots you. But it's so much more prideful if you can take something and leave it conspicuously....

So when I heard these women talking about me behind me, I thought I had been discovered. I almost fainted when one tapped me on the shoulder and said she wanted to talk to me. The first thing she said was that I had brought the best food to the bazaar, and it was a shame I hadn't brought more than the two loaves because they were already gone. One of her friends had bought them and she offered this lady a taste....

Well, it turned out that I was asked to come to the church in the next block the next weekend and make more, with her providing all of the ingredients. They sold dozens of loaves. Then I began to wake up and smell the money. If they could make a profit, why should I be giving my breads away just for the exchange of other food? So I went around to all the churches and said I'd make the breads in their kitchens for their affairs for so much a loaf, with them providing the ingredients, and I got a circuit of churches and private parties now. It's not much of a business yet, but I had to get a Post Office Box to make sure people could contact me, and I just had cards made up to pass around. You can guess that I'm trying to write down every recipe that we made when I was a kid! I'm going to add the soups to go with the breads, and the jellies that we made from the fruit and veggies that were left over. Then there's the pie crusts that we made from the stale crumbs of the breads....

While Maggie and Hilda are happy with their own small businesses, Nancy (age 54, Boothbay, Maine, 1976) began to think in terms of expanding of her newly created cottage industry:

> I can live in this old mobile home in the off-season, but in a week or so I'll have to move out to the woods to a shed which was used to store bait. The owners will arrive for the summer. They let me stay here in exchange for not letting the kids vandalize it, and part of that is charity, because the owners also let me use the electric heater....
>
> You can see that I don't have lots of room, but what I do have is filled with the flora that grows in the marshes on Southport and down on the Bath peninsula. I get rides from a couple of fishermen who have trucks, and I just spend the day collecting while they fish or chat. They haul these back for me, and you can see I barely can fit it all in!....
>
> Most of these sedges and rushes and reed mares will be woven into mats and wreaths and baskets by the time the tourists come in droves in July and August. This will be my first big year, and I'm excited. I never knew that anyone would buy this ratty stuff that I hated all my life. Not that I don't find them rather pretty; they are. But I had to gather it when I was a kid, and I wanted to be out playing with the other children. My mother and aunts made table mats from these for Christmas presents, and it was my job to do all the dirty work.
>
> I was thinking about how few items I make. I'll bet there are other women who could work with me to make this a much bigger business. For instance, Sally, over to Bath—near the Iron Works—makes the most beautiful little metal objects out of pieces that she finds in their scrap, and they would look great as part of the structure of my wreaths and baskets. And Dorothy over to Small Point makes gorgeous cushions out of old materials. Now those would go just fine with the chairs that Jack Perkins makes. He lives in an old fishing shack near the wharf and hasn't got a dime. But does

he ever take an ax and make the most of a short fall—and does absolute wonders with some old tools and sandpaper. I haven't seen better looking ladderbacks in the stores. He could use the help of a younger person, though, since he is getting on. . . .

When I come to think on it, we've got a group here of hard-up people that could be coming together to make a decent year-round business. Now why didn't I think of this last week?

Nancy probably did not think of it because she had not been sharing her thoughts with anyone. If she had been in a situation wherein women were telling their life stories, someone would have said a "magic word" which would have inspired brainstorming on the subject of a cooperative venture. Think about the opportunities afforded by the presence of a church and its membership: a place to meet and people with whom to share experiences and dreams.

Before I left that year, Nancy and some of her acquaintances had met on neutral ground—a flea market—and talked about forming a co-op. I was told that the following summer, Nancy and three other crafters were renting space in a store on the tourist-trade Route 1 and sharing the living space of an attic in a nearby house. They were still "homeless," but they were pooling their talents and their company; together they must have found some measure of success. (Unfortunately, I did not have an opportunity to track their progress.)

Camaraderie also can result in a more permanent bonding: a gathering of homeless individuals to form a small community. This type of communal living and working situation is exemplified in the formation of what was called The Shearers and Spinners in the late 1970s in Pennsylvania between Philadelphia and New Hope. I thought TSAS was just a store selling sheepskins, but after an hour of chitchat I discovered that much more was going on. Several homeless women and men had been using a barn as a place to live while bartering their skills for sheepskins and wool. After a few sales and the "gift" of a very old house in terrible condition, the group practically rebuilt the house and created a store in which to sell their handmade vests, coats, slippers, etc. (from the skins) and sweaters, capes, and scarves (from the wool). Another homeless person moved in who knew how to build machinery by which further production could be accomplished. A year later another homeless woman had joined the community and she was making and selling homemade baked goods. By the time I left the region, there was an antiques shop added to the communal effort, and the machinist was looking for a partner to create a repair shop.

I came here one day completely disoriented from not eating or sleeping regularly. About all I could do was to ask for some food. The next thing I knew I was sitting in a warm barn drinking hot, thick soup and eating cornbread. Every once in a while someone came by and asked if I needed a blanket or more soup. I think I slept for two days straight . . . .

They were an odd bunch, but they had more in common than not, and by putting together their abilities and desire not to perish, they started with just sheer hope—no pun intended—and hard work. I have been part of their sharing now for almost eight months, and I'm in charge of the antiques shop. My husband and I were dealers for years, and when he left me for another woman I sort of went downhill, drinking and taking drugs and such. But now I'm going to make it, and I'm going to stay with these terrific people, all of them who began over again like I have. If I hadn't been able to share my story with them, I would have just kept it bottled up and drowned myself in its slop. When I started to talk about all of my misadventures, I found that they all had similar problems, and this is like a giant support group. You know, not so much in size, but like a little church of some kind. . . .

You know, no one in any agency gave a hot damn about my being screwed legally and becoming homeless. It took other people who were also down on their luck to understand how I felt and to give me what I needed: a chance to be part of a family—and to be part of the working force again. It wouldn't hurt the social workers to take a look at what we do. They wouldn't care, though, and we both know that. It's a system, and a lousy one at that. There isn't any opportunity to work. All they can offer is the address of a mission where they hand you a meal once a day. Most of us women who are homeless don't want a dole; we want a place in society again. And we know how to work for it. We all have some ability, but you'd never know it from the attitude of the social workers. No wonder we don't want to even go into their offices. . . .

The special bonding offered by "family" settings offsets the rejection by spouse and/or social service or legal system providers, stimulating personal growth as well as enhancing the group. Reentry into the economic structure is even more radically exemplified by an examination of H.O.M.E. (Homeworkers Organized for More Employment) in Orland, Maine, which has been in existence since 1970. Abbé Pierre (his name as a priest in the French Resistance during World War II) describes H.O.M.E. and its mission (in the Winter 1988: 7 issue of *This Time*, a newspaper produced by the community members) as:

a community formed among people once desperate, often without hope, who have found hope helping one another. The economic philosophy of H.O.M.E. will not be taught in the economics department of [universities]. . . H.O.M.E.'s founder, Lucy Poulin, has been slowly implementing her economic philosophy over the past eighteen years: use natural resources and native skills to build a local economy. The co-op started with crafts, selling the products of cottage industry and teaching the necessary skills from raising sheep and carding wool to leather working. Last year more than $250,000.00 of crafts were sold. . . . What we all share is the certainty that what life requires from us, as in a family, is that the smallest, the weakest is served first. If that doesn't happen, then the family dies.

When I first encountered the members of H.O.M.E. there were only two typical farm-type buildings. As the years progressed more structures were built and continuing entrepreneurship was evident. The community now includes retail craft and food shops; daycare center; learning center and college program; flea market; sawmill; shingle mill; auto repair shop; horse training; shelter building and other workshops; distribution centers for food, fuel, clothing, and farm animals; transportation program; medical and legal assistance; co-ops for food, clothing, animals, etc.; museum; newspaper; homes built by and/or for the residents; and shelters for the abused and homeless. Everyone partakes of the emotional and economic benefits; they all recognize that without H.O.M.E., almost all would be in dire circumstances. General manager Nancy Upton says: "I realize how lucky I am to be able to live freely, have a home and family, and not worry about being thrown into the street" (1986: 9).

What Abbé Pierre did not emphasize is that Lucy Poulin is an ex-nun who has never relinquished her Christian commitment to serve others. Sister Lucy was instrumental in conjoining H.O.M.E. (a secular group) with St. Francis Community. She has utilized a community land trust to acquire property and provide lifetime housing rights to those who would not otherwise be able to own a home. When Sister Lucy began her journey into social responsibility, other churchwomen joined her in donations, volunteerism, and spirit. Now, almost twenty years later, she is surrounded by women and families who have literally built a community together. Religious women come to H.O.M.E. to gain inspiration; they may spend a day, a month, or their lives there, freely committing themselves to serving others while realizing the true meaning of joy. What Sister Lucy has done (consciously or unconsciously) is to use Mary as a role model: she gave up her own "security" to begin a venture in faith without knowing how it would end; she worked with others in mutual support to fulfill a commitment and create "community"; and she has been willing to be a sometimes unwelcome voice in a world not convinced that the poor, uneducated, battered, old, ill, and oppressed are worth all of the effort she (and her colleagues) puts forth. Sister Lucy is a visionary who began as a neighborhood churchwoman who wasn't afraid to take a step in faith. For Lucy, that first step was joining with the poorest of rural women to sell homemade crafts in a rundown farmhouse. While H.O.M.E. is a rural organization dedicated to maximizing human services and managing the land (through the establishment of the Covenant Community Land Trust)—and thus providing the greatest opportunities for personal benefits, homes, employment, and fellowship —this model of a cooperative venture and community land trust is applicable to the urban experience.

The Community Land Cooperative of Cincinnati exemplifies how an urban land trust deals with the particular problems that affect the residents of cities which face land/property speculation and preservation activities which so often lead to the poor being displaced as a neighborhood is restored beyond its former inhabitants' ability to remain—either as tenants or owners. (This phenomenon is known as gentrification.) Responding to one woman's immediate need for a home for herself and ten children, the West End Alliance of Churches and Ministries—an organization comprised rather obviously of the committed religious—created a land trust situation in which option money was made available by the Revolving Loan Fund of the Institute for Community Economics (in Massachusetts). When other properties came up for sale that were appropriate for single or multiple dwellings, the CLCC acquired property for those who would not otherwise be eligible for equity. Two prominent members of the CLCC were Sisters Barbara Wheeler and Monica McGloin of the Dominican Sisters of the Sick Poor. They believed that poor people who have never actualized feelings of personal power over their lives need to become very involved in the workings of a co-op in order to learn not only for themselves, but to pass that knowledge along to others. Consequently, disparate players in one neighborhood shared past experiences, current problems, and future-oriented responsibilities, resulting in both a *sense* of community and a *physical* community.

What can the average churchwoman do to assist pre-homeless and homeless women at the very lowest (neighborhood) level of organizing? First, she is the only one who can actually *locate* them! If all she can do is place posters in malls, coffee shops, and drugstores that announce a church bazaar which will provide free food and clothing, then she has performed well; she will bring someone into the church who would undoubtedly not be there otherwise. She can create situations for sharing experiences which reveal personal needs to be fulfilled. She can be responsible for finding space (for sleeping, eating, talking, and business), offering needed raw materials for cottage industries, creating purchasing power by advertising new business, showcasing new products, and taking requests for classes in particular crafts which can be taught by the homeless artists. At the higher levels of organizing, the mainstream churchwoman can be actively engaged in studying real estate patterns as preparation for creating a self-sufficiency community, whether it be by a deliberately researched and planned effort of a community land trust, or foundation/corporation or government sponsorship. In all matters, what is important is that political strength is garnered through becoming involved as a committed group. "Political power" is a necessary force from several standpoints.

3. From the Shadows of Political Power

"Political power" and "assistance" have multiple meanings. In one sense, it really is necessary to focus on that kind of assistance which is proudly proclaimed by politicians and service providers as available and in practice in our communities: the socially responsible activities that ensure equal treatment and justice for all. What can the local churchwoman do when she realizes that women are being victimized by the very individuals and systems which are established to prevent or eliminate such unjust treatment? Marty (age 57, Santa Monica, California, 1988) comments on one interesting solution:

> I guess everyone thinks I've always been down and out. Boy, are they wrong! I was a householder in three states and was always part of the community action. I remember one time we were—us house owners, I mean—we were worried

about some developers moving in and buying up property and we heard that they were planning to put up a hospital complex for the criminally insane... And we found out that a couple of our so-called honest politicians were involved in some zoning changes that would let that happen. They just happened to be part of the developers' group... Hah! Just happened to be.... So I—and a couple of neighbors—started a petition to get a town meeting going. We wanted to get the men out there and get questioned by the people that voted them in.

So we got everyone in a turmoil and people were really for this town meeting. . . . At the last minute the politicians made sure that there couldn't be a town meeting where they could be questioned on a one-on-one basis. You can bet they were afraid of being found out. But I can't think of a better way to make the powers that be own up to what they do... just look at the scandals all over the place. Washington. Mayors. District attorneys. All those lawyers who lie for each other. There's nothing getting better, either. We're told that there's places for us to stay for free, free lawyers to protect us and compensation money for crime victims.

But there's lots of lies. I'd like to see some of those lies come out in the town meetings where the liars have a terrible punishment at the hands of the victims...

Can't you see the politicians working all day—like doing grave digging—and having to give the money right to the people who voted them in and got screwed?

Churchwomen can insist that local politicians follow through with campaign promises and declared victim/homeless assistance programs and services. These politicians and their appointees live (and often worship) in the district, their children (usually) go to local schools, their wives shop in the area, and with a united voice from community churchwomen, people voted into office can be held accountable for their attitudes and actions. Because women often feel isolated from politics and politicians, it is easy to buy into the notion that one is powerless. But that is not so; it just sometimes takes "more than one" to raise a voice and be heard. The community church is the place to network and correlate complaints with activism; that building can be offered as a place for a town meeting, for such open forums are not restricted to the New England village town hall. It will not be surprising that people support the initiative—and have quite a list of complaints to put on the agenda. Where similar opportunities have been implemented, agendas have been long and represent a variety of complaints.

One major complaint of homeless people relates to the need for a legal address before one qualifies for certain monies and the right to vote. Dorine (age 58, Mystic, Connecticut, 1979) had an ingenious solution:

> If I don't have a legal address, how the hell am I going to *vote* for someone who may be trying to help us homeless? There are all kinds of restrictions on me because I don't have that legal address. The missions don't count. My car doesn't count. My post office box doesn't count. It seems to me that if there was a way for us to be part of making suggestions without the stigma of being called homeless and therefore stupid or drugged-out, we would have enough in numbers to vote for different politicians. . . .

> Now if I could put my car on a lot with a listed legal address and call that my house, I could be just as legal as the person on the next lot with a street number. A trailer is pretty close to a mobile home; it's a matter of fixing it up on the outside to look like an established home. So a trailer can be a legal address. I don't see why my car is much different. . . . And if I can't use my car, well, why can't I use the White House. . . I could move to D.C.

> Haven't we been paying taxes all these years to pay for its upkeep? It seems to me that it belongs to all the people, so why can't I use it as my address? All homeless people should put it down and be able to get their mail there. It's only right. The president only stays there for a short time

and yet he gets to use it legal. And most of the really rich men never pay any taxes at all! I know I paid more taxes in my time than most of the big company executives and the politicians. . . .

A recent (November 4, 1989) article in the *Los Angeles Times* reports that "courts" (it doesn't specify which courts) have "ordered New York and other cities to allow the homeless to register to vote." There is still a requirement that a homeless person provide a mailing address, but apparently a post office box or a social service agency is now sufficient. This is a signficant change in attitude and law, but it still will not cover all situations in which a legal address is necessary for payments, nor will it help those who travel constantly while seeking a job or inexpensive place to live. Here is a way for a churchwoman to assist a homeless woman. If every churchmember would "adopt" a homeless woman by allowing her the use of an address for mailing purposes, there would be no need for her to be rejected in any particular situation in which a legal address is required. I suppose that the argument against this is that one might be afraid that the person would come, uninvited, to the front door, and it is a legitimate concern. Perhaps the solution to that concern is for churchwomen to meet with particular homeless women and select one whom they feel they can trust not to invade their privacy. The church is an ideal meeting place for women to start a "talking" relationship, especially while sharing a meal. In other cases, there does not seem to be any reason why a convent, rectory, or seminary address would not be acceptable: they are residences.

In another sense, assistance means the accessibility of the legal and judicial systems. The lack of ability to utilize these public sector systems denotes being in the shadows of political power. Concepts and issues need to be addressed. The first is *indemnification.* While restitution has become a popular term, and the process of restitution to victims of crime has been instituted in some states (most often through the court system) with varying degrees of limited success, restitution is not indemnification. Restitution requires that a victimizer pays a victim for finalized injury-related expenses. Expenses may include a present need—such as plastic surgery—but basically restitution is meant to reimburse the victim for a loss or damage that has been sustained. What is not considered, and is expressed by victims almost as litany, is the provision for needs which may not be known at the time of compensation—insurance, so to speak, for the future; indemnification is restitution plus the assurance—the means—for a woman's future. To exemplify the necessity for indemnification, Beth (age 57, Baltimore, Maryland, 1979) had no idea that agreeing to a (lump sum) settlement to meet her immediate need for rental monies instead of insisting on continuing payments to meet future needs would result in homelessness:

> Allan had cheated on me once too often, and he knew that I was going to get a divorce. So when his lawyer suggested what I thought was a generous offer to pay me a lump sum for my first and last month rents and all of the moving costs, and quite a bit to put in the bank for interest purposes, I thought I would be ahead of the game. I didn't have a lawyer of my own since Allan made a point that we could save money by using just one to represent us both, and I had no idea that I was being a fool. I thought that Allan was being punished for cheating on me and he was being decent by giving me plenty of money up front to make up for his adultery—not dribble out little bits to me so that I'd always be looking for the next dime. . . .
>
> I had been a housewife for over twenty years and let's face it, my honed skills were limited to cleaning, cooking, shopping, and taking care of kids. I never thought about Social Security—and that I wouldn't get any! Allan was to give me money for medical insurance for five years, and I was so dumb that I thought that was good. Of course I figured by then that I'd either get a job or get married again, even though now I know that neither was logical. . . .
>
> So ten years later, here I am without any money and without any ever to come. I can't go back and ask for more; I was a dead woman the minute I signed that agreement that only

paid me for an awful past and my immediate needs and didn't consider that I'd live longer than nine years. I don't qualify for anything except welfare, and I lived for too many years as an upper-middle-class lady. I can't rent an apartment on welfare, and I have to go downtown to charity clinics for medical care. I need surgery, and I don't even have a place to live.

Someone ought to warn women not to go for the quick money, but to think about the fact that they don't have any future without proper planning if they don't have a job and some kind of benefits to come in. Why isn't there any publicity that reaches women before they sign away their lives? Why aren't men forced to pay alimony that is really an unemployment check?

No woman should be without her own lawyer! He is the clue to receiving the equivalent of Social Security. No one should have to end up homeless and dead while her ex-husband, the one who done her wrong, lives in luxury.

Repeatedly, I have heard stories about women not having attorneys to represent them. The basic theme is that a lawyer who is a friend of the husband's has told them that it is not necessary and money will be saved by utilizing the services of just one attorney. Variations on the theme are threats which make it impossible for the woman to obtain a personal legal representative. The results are the same: the man retains his gainful employment with lifetime benefits and other monies and properties while building on a base which assures a pleasant retirement, and the woman sustains continuing losses which result in a downward spiraling of lifestyle and eventual homelessness. Sally (age 55, Baltimore, Maryland, 1977) notes not only the lack of indemnification, but the important issue of unethical behavior by lawyers:

> The lawyer was his old friend, but I thought that he was telling the truth when he said we could save a lot of money by him representing both of us. I didn't object to that until it was too late and I saw the papers that he handed to me to

sign. Why, the house, the cars, the furniture, the bonds—everything went to Harry and I got a piddling amount as a settlement. I said I wouldn't sign such a document. And then I got threatened: "You'll get nothing," they said, "we know how to do that."

I couldn't hire a lawyer then because Harry had wiped out our joint accounts, putting them in his name only, I'm sure, in some other bank. There I was, living from day to day in a house that I had lovingly scrimped for for twenty-one years, and I'm told that Harry gets it all.

I didn't know that it is illegal to have one lawyer handle a divorce for two people in Maryland. Oh, maybe there are exceptions, like when there isn't anything to divide up or something, but certainly not in a case where the people are fighting over what they should get.

But I know it now and the Bar Association won't do anything about it. We need to have an open discussion of things like this that women can get to and just yell out what happened—and let the lawyers explain to everyone in town what they did. No Bar guys deciding what to do. Just good old-fashioned "you did it" and if he can't give a good excuse, then he's out of the legal profession right then and there. . . .

There aren't any lawyers in Maryland who will take a case like mine after the wife has practically given up any right to go to the police and complain that she has been beaten for years. She's not being beaten any more. So there she is, meaning me, and I'm told to pack up my clothes and get the hell out. I kept having those papers shoved in front of me until I needed the small settlement so bad just because I needed a car. So I signed. The lawyer poured drinks for him and my husband, and they toasted each other while I sat there crying. . . . I keep thinking that I should strangle that lawyer before I jump off the beltway bridge. . . .

Every state has a Bar Association which has a monitoring system. Homeless women express how that system is either inadequate or just plain corrupt in many states. Jane (age 52, Baltimore, Maryland, 1978) offers some interesting solutions:

When I found out that Frank's lawyer lied to me about what I was allowed to have, I told him that I was going to report him for unethical behavior. He just laughed and said to go ahead. He said if I had been stupid enough to let him handle my interests also, then it was my fault that I got nothing. You know, I didn't realize that one lawyer couldn't handle both sides of a divorce. The lawyer said he could, and then when I complained, he said that he couldn't, that he was only my husband's lawyer. So where the hell was mine, I wanted to know. He just laughed again.

I complained to the Maryland Attorney Grievance Commission, but a lawyer called the Bar Counsel and then sent me a letter saying there was no basis for my complaint. He never said anything about it being illegal for a lawyer to handle both sides of a problem divorce. He just ignored it. So who is watching the AGC? No one, I'll bet. There was no one for me to complain to about the Bar Counsel's decision. After years of searching for some kind of resolution, and by then I was living with an old man just to have a room to live in, I found out that the Court of Appeals has jurisdiction over complaints against lawyers. But there's no way for the poor woman to get there, especially if she couldn't get a lawyer to represent her in the first place!

Now I figured out what's wrong here. First, there's no way for a woman to know she's been lied to by an attorney because the legal profession keeps its little secrets about what they can get away with. Those secrets should be posted in large print on library bulletin boards. Second, there should be a way for victims to get their complaints to a commission that isn't made up of a bunch of lawyers who protect each other. We ought to know who these damn men are and get to them publicly if we need to. Their names and backgrounds should be public knowledge, and we should be able to renounce them and they'd have to answer the charges. Third, all these thieves—and that's what they are when they steal a woman's future—should be forced to provide free legal services to make sure that every woman who wants a divorce can get into court with professional representation. And they'd better do their darn best, because if they lose, they support the woman and her kids. Fourth, every one of them should have his name emblazoned on a public building as a punishment. Fifth, every woman who has been screwed by a lawyer should be allowed to live in his house—at his expense, forever. Sixth, how about hiring victims to fill the jobs that deal with victimization? I don't know of any ex- or still-victims getting jobs which they know something about. It always seems to be someone's friend who doesn't know diddly-squat about what it feels like to be a victim that gets hired for these new jobs that supposedly deal with victims' rights and putting things right. It's probably why there are so many things still wrong with all the systems! Put a *personally* committed person in a job!

Does any of this make sense to you? Something's got to be done to stop this illegal behavior, and it's for damn sure that the lawyers aren't going to do anything about it. Women have to have a future too, and the men stick together like glue. And when you get a woman who's made it, why she's worse than the men; she has to prove to herself that she's got male power.

Lawyers and judges have also been (unofficially) charged with engaging in collusive behavior which has resulted in a woman becoming homeless. It is important that one recognizes that the charges are always unofficial; there is no way for the indigent victim to *officially* charge any officer of the court. The victim is left to allege misconduct to a state's attorney or prosecutor; it is up to that public servant to pursue the matter. Again, women charge that officials protect each other. Sue (age 39, Baltimore, Maryland) was hitchhiking along I-83 to York, Pennsylvania (and beyond) when a friend and I picked her up in 1978.

I didn't have a chance. The lawyer who was representing my husband was grossly incompetent, but he was related by marriage to the judge. I don't know if that's illegal or not, but it sure did make a difference to me and any future I might have had. *My* wonderful wimp of a lawyer knew he was whipped when he saw how things were going. Everything he said was overruled. During a break he told me that he had three more cases coming up before the same judge and couldn't make him angry, so he was just taking it easy. By the time he had finished presenting my case, I looked like I was just plain bitchy! I wouldn't have recognized my own life if I hadn't been the boob who was the plaintiff. . . .

I asked for the house, the children, a car, and support. Guess what I got? I got the children—who he didn't want from the beginning—but not a place to put them or money to do more than feed them a few times a week. My husband got the expensive house, the two cars, and a new life. Now what could I do for those kids? I couldn't keep them with me. I had to hand them over to their grandparents so that they could go to school, have a home, and wear clothes.

If I can get a job in Pennsylvania maybe I'll be able to send for them. Sometime. But I only have experience in working in factory outlet stores, and the only place around here that has those is in PA. You can't get a job without experience, and I need more than minimum wage or I can't get a place to live. There isn't enough child support for that. . . .

Now didn't the judge know that I needed more than what I got? Of course he did. But he made sure that my husband's lawyer got every chance to make me look like a really self-sufficient babe with a brilliant future in sales. So I wouldn't need any money, or a car, or a house. It was just shameful.

I asked my lawyer to challenge the judge's decision. He almost vomited. So I went to the courthouse and hit every official, and then I went to Legal Aid, and then I went to the Bar Association's lawyer referral service, and then I complained to their grievance committee. You can guess the results. Here I am, with everything I own in my bags in your car heading for PA and the outlet stores. Not one public official would tackle a case against that judge. Maybe he's related to all of them, but I think the better answer is that they all cover ass for each other. I'd like to see that judge explain to the whole community how successful I am and how I'm supposed to raise those kids on no alimony and fifty bucks a week child support. That guy was voted in, and the people who voted for him ought to know how he works in court. Not only that, but there ought to be a public explanation of my complaint that he plays favors among lawyers. Let him tell everyone in the voting area how his relative wins his cases. Mine certainly wasn't on merit, and I quote you that from one of the people in the audience who had sat through my case. When a person can't hire an attorney to make a complaint against a judge, how else can we get attention? Are we supposed to attack him physically so we get into the newspapers?

Going one step further, Betty (age 56, Baltimore, Maryland, 1978) has a plan (which is similar to others that have been expressed by victims) to eliminate collusion and corruption between public officers:

I was so angry that no one would investigate my charges that my husband's lawyer was unethical and probably broke laws along with the court officer who lied to keep me from my own trial that I set up a booth on the street and talked with people as they passed by. Before the police made me go away, I got some good ideas from other people who are just as irate as I am. We all seem to know that corruption is widespread, but there isn't anything we can do about it.

Okay, we start with the idea that people do care about the way our public officials act, and that we don't like it. It's now up to the cities to come to a decision: corruption forever or people standing up for their supposed rights. How can we do it? Simple. Every city is divided into voting areas. Every politician is attached to an area and responsible to the people who vote for him. Twice a year he has to defend himself. There are public meetings in public buildings, and every person who has a charge prepares it in advance—on paper—and it is given to the politician so that he has time to prepare his answers. At the biannual meetings, the politician must address every issue, and where particular cases are brought up, he has to make the time to publicly talk about each one. It may take a week, but that's what he is going to have to do as part of his job. Now everyone in the city knows where his candidates really stand, not just mouth-off about.

That ought to stop collusion and corruption. It might even solve all of our crime problems, since some of it comes from the activities of the officials and the rest from the examples they set for the people in their districts. The people would love it!

What can the local churchwoman do to assist pre-homeless and homeless women in relation to access to and utilization of our legal and judicial systems? Connie (age 54, Los Angeles, California, 1988) recalls how women worked for "causes" in her own hometown church in Virginia.

I remember when I was a member of just about every committee in our little Lutheran church. We only had about 220 members, and most of them didn't show regularly, but we sure did get a lot done. We had fairs to raise money for an orphanage in England, we collected clothes for the needy in the Midwest during floodtimes, and we baked until our arms were sore for money to buy canned goods for tornado victims in Indiana—or maybe it was Missouri. Someone always showed up to tell a story about people in need, and we'd get together and figure out how to come to their aid. Everyone had some skill to offer. Some women were just naturally good at collecting things from people who never gave anything, some women were great at getting money from the stingiest in the community, and some were terrific at making sure that everyone had all the tables and chairs and silverware—you know—had everything on the spot when and where it was needed. . . .

We had a few women who were always working for a cause. Before it was popular, we had two women who were what might be called courtroom advocates. They stuck their noses into everybody's business, but they were right there when a woman needed help in getting a lawyer and sitting through a sticky court case. Why, I remember one time when a widow was about to lose her house and she couldn't get a lawyer for free. These two gals went out on a limb and sat in every law office in town until they scared-up a man to represent her. And then they sat in court with her every day, giving her moral support. I think they spent a lot of time just explaining what was going on because the lawyer really didn't spend any unnecessary time on her. . . .

Where are all of these women now? I pass by churches that are full on Sundays, but I don't see too many fairs these days. I read a lot of newspapers because there isn't too much else I can do for free. I see organizations listed in long columns and they are always looking for volunteers, but I don't see any saying they are starting centers for the neighborhood needy.

If only I could tell my story in church—and other stories would come out—I could have a committee going in a month and there wouldn't be any of us having to shoplift to get something to wear or eat. We'd have a jobbing network, too.

But I'm not welcome anywhere, even in a plain church. Everyone is all dressed up or at least has shoes without holes. And where could I leave my things? In the minister's office? Big joke. They even lock the churches now. Heaven forbid that any of *us* get in. . . .

Amy (age 49, Santa Monica, California, 1987) also feels the need to return to church. She presently belongs to a support group which is coordinated by the minister's wife. Amy was particularly impressed with the ability of the women in the group to "jump in" and fill in stories with their own experiences. Scholars would call this "sharing a perceptual paradigm." All that means is that when people share a common background, experiences, and knowledge, they have the ability to understand easily what the others are saying, leading to interruptions of similar details which fit the original storyline.

I have been alone for so long, just dwelling on this matter so much and going nearly nuts in the process, that when I was in the group with the other women and heard my own story, well, I just couldn't have been happier. I wasn't alone anymore. I didn't even have to hear the whole stories; I could fill in the middle and ending with my own experiences. . . .

If only I had had this opportunity three years ago. I wouldn't have been so miserable, thinking that I was probably the only one going through this. Maybe if we could have talked about these things then I wouldn't have ended up on the street. Just think, June doesn't have to run away and try to change her identity. We've all shared how it just isn't possible. . . .

Did anyone here not interrupt poor June? She never really did get to finish! Let's give her a chance to get it all out. Okay? Then we'll all jump in again and see how all of these things come from the same problems in the legal system. It seems that we all have come up with a better scheme that the City Attorney's Office has!

Using the church as a place for support group meetings has an added advantage: there is a kitchen where food can be kept refrigerated, warmed, and from which it can be served. The preparation and sharing of food is an aesthetic event, one traditional in nature and encompassing pleasure, custom, ritual, impromptu joking, and storytelling. In the case of many decision-making sessions, a potluck dinner has enhanced productivity while encouraging sociability—a networking opportunity. Clare (age 59, Westminster, Maryland, 1979) recognized the impact of food on sociability and organizing:

When I was in the chips, my favorite day was Sunday. After church we ladies got together in the big hall for a potluck lunch that lasted all afternoon. The men always said we got together to gossip, but while we were getting our tables set up properly and arranged by salads, sandwiches, casseroles, fruits, and then desserts, we were exchanging the important news of the week. Then we made a great fuss about filling our plates with first one type of food and then another, and commenting on how wonderful everything looked so that everyone was feeling proud about their platters. . . .

There was always this fuss about who would sit where, and we always ended up sitting beside the same people as if it were a great surprise. We would taste one item after another and in-between all of the tasting and commenting on the dishes, there was this negotiating for what would be the main topic of the day. Sometimes it was a foreign affair, or a Washington scandal, or a local one, or something that needed to be done in a hurry, or something that needed planning well in advance—like the annual harvest ham dinner, or the winterfest. . . or bull or oyster roast.

By maybe four o'clock we could have made arrangements to change the world, but the men still made fun of us; we had been gossiping. I think about those days a lot. I don't think I've ever quite enjoyed myself as I did on Sundays. Of course now my Sundays are just like any other day. I can't go anywhere different, even though I have tried to go to some of the local churches. They just don't have the spirit we did, and when there's a ladies' group, you know that I'm not going to be welcome. I don't belong to the church because I can't afford to. And I certainly don't get any personal invitations; I don't have a phone or even an address. But I wonder what the women do now in the church. I don't see them hanging around after services; they leave as fast as they can. There must be little standing committees that meet at night for an hour or so somewhere. That's not half the fun of the making of a committee and planning for something special. These people look at things as chores. We had fun with our causes. . . .

If I could be in a church again, I'd like to see the Sunday brunches back again, and this time I'd make sure that we focused on doing some social good. I mean really important good, like sponsoring a place for women like me—and I see a lot of us wandering around the malls and stores all day and in movies most nights. We could even be responsible for making the churches the places for nighttime slumber palaces. There they are, just empty houses of God, and there could be cots put up at night. . . and all those unused rooms would be signals to God that people care.

It wouldn't take much more than a couple of Sunday potlucks to solve the traffic and parking problems that the council people keep arguing about. And what would be even better would be to have every second Sunday set aside for a group-church potluck day. Then we ladies could tackle the really big issues. If all the women who belong to churches get others who don't to come to regular potluck meetings, why we could set up a network of church-sponsored houses across the country and take care of all the women who need everything from food to housing.

Oh, to be arranging platters of ham, potato salads and cole slaw between the pretty green and red aspics, and smelling the warm desserts at the end of the table, wondering how much you could save aside before anyone noticed. . . .

I think Clare made many salient points about the "power" of church-related functions. Every churchwoman should be able to see herself in some role in Clare's scenario.

Paula (age 39, Los Angeles, California, 1987), Sandy (age 43, Santa Monica, California, 1987), and Colleen (age 46, Los Angeles, California, 1987) were only three of the women in the support group of seven for battered women who had ideas to share over sandwiches and coffee. This group was started by two battered women who were dissatisfied with the local group sponsored by a community center. "The women just weren't given the chance to come up with any constructive plans," said Paula. "We were told to talk about our problems as if we were in a counseling or therapy session, and we wanted to get down to business and change the system."

Wouldn't you like to see every slumlord having to put up truly terrific housing for the poor instead of paying fines which go into some city council or court drawer? Can't you just see the embezzlers of old ladies' trust funds getting their hands dirty plastering walls in the new housing? And how about those repugnant public officials who take money under the table for their campaigns having to spend their weekends making arrangements for each poor family to move in? The lawyers who make sure that all of their male friends have plenty to live on can spend their nights and weekends locating the wives that are now homeless and getting them back into the courtroom for some equal treatment. I'd like to see the city attorney who told me I had to testify against John buying my food and clothes.

Here is how Sandy answered the question, 'Who would you like to see doing what?':

We're here from Ohio, and the worst thing I can think of is the banker who forecloses on your farm just so some big corporation can come in and add big bucks to the bank's coffers. Al didn't start to treat me like this until we lost everything, and I know that he is taking out on me what he'd like to do to the men who took away his whole life. . . .

You know, if we had had the chance to get some light industry going on the farm, we wouldn't have had to go bankrupt from the loss of our crops. I'd like to see the bankers be in charge of finding us other people who have something they could contribute to the farm communities which are hard pressed to survive. I know of one family in Tennessee who gave up part of their farm to another family so that they could combine their knowledge. The last I heard was that they were using the farmland to feed all of them and the rest of the land for a small factory which they built themselves. Would you believe they're making wooden skiffs and selling them to all the fancy lakefront people?

I [Colleen] know of a farm family who had to split up because of a forced auction. They are from Kentucky, and the wife is out here somewhere trying to find a commune she can get into. I met her out at LAX when we were both watching for luggage that had been left by the telephones. Her husband is a total drunk now and has disappeared, but she told me that he was the finest breeder of horses she knew, and all he needed was to get into partnership with someone who could train gaited horses properly, and then he could show a few, win, and get a backer. I grew up on five-gaited horses. I could train them as well as any man. If only I could find him. I know a man who'd back that sort of venture, but I never thought it would be me who would be interested. . . .

How about taxing all the racetrack owners who make over a certain amount a bit to give to the communities they're in? I'll bet that enough money could be raised to start businesses for women who know how to do something but are living on the skids in the area. Oh wait! Why not get some legislation passed that will give a penny for every dollar spent at the racetrack to a company of women who'll get to do all the food making and serving at the track?

All of these women are pre-homeless, knowing that at any time they may be forced from their homes by abusive husbands and have no place to go. They choose to stay because their alternatives are worse than having their husbands "whistle [their] way through six weeks of battering-behavior counseling by a woman they laugh at because it's obvious that she's not even into men" (Debra, age 41, Los Angeles, California, 1987). But they are not just complaining; they are suggesting innovative ideas for solving some of the societal problems that still puzzle the professionals! Churchwomen on the local level could be sponsoring such sessions and working with these women to put ideas into action. Interestingly, Sandy and Colleen touched upon the same topics (self-sufficiency and a return to the small family farm) that the nation's Roman Catholic bishops did during their November (1989) meeting (to celebrate the 200th anniversary of the Catholic hierarchy in the United States) in Baltimore. Since the policies of the Church are in some agreement with the suggestions made by homeless women, there would seem to be no reason for local parishes to object to furthering discussion on such subjects as shared housing, cottage industry, community building, small-farm development and in general, calling for attention to human rights issues and social causes.

But what if the stories that the women tell reveal really unusual—even frightening—experiences? Is the mainstream churchwoman able to remain composed and open-minded—and understand? Why not? There are mainstream women who are psychologists, sociologists, folklorists, anthropologists, nurses, and doctors. If the women of any small church feel the need to invite a particular professional into a support group, there are certainly members from their own or a neighboring church who would oblige. (That is what networking is: making contacts and providing mutual benefits.) One of the most needed services for pre-homeless and homeless women is an outlet for sharing experiences. It is within the informality of talking about particular issues that the "unexpected" appears, and those experiences are the ones which, kept silenced, may cause psychic impairment or dysfunctional behaviors. With a support group which focuses on incidents related to victimization, topics such as haggings, near-death and out-of-body experiences, religious visitations, etc., might emerge. The telling of these incidents is the beginning of healing. Alcoholics Anonymous is a well-known association which recognizes the therapeutic aspect of storytelling. If we listen carefully to the stories that homeless women tell, we can better understand why some of them have been labelled "mentally ill" and how that *label* has led to their current condition.

4. From the Shadows of the Mind

Bea (age 48, Los Angeles, California, 1984) was committed to a mental institution after stabbing her doctor with a knife:

> I've only been out on my own for three weeks now. I was supposed to go live with a cousin, but she left for Hawaii and locked up the house, and I don't know when she'll be back. I told the doctor I'm supposed to see, but he didn't seem to be listening to me. No one ever did, so I shouldn't be surprised. . . .

> See, I didn't really try to kill that doctor. And I certainly didn't know he was *my* doctor! I had had my appendix out and wasn't coming along that well when I had a coughing fit and thought I was dying. I pushed the nurse's bell, and then, according to the doctors, I was dead for a very short time. They had paddles on me and stuff and shocked me back to life. But that's not what I remember, and when I told everyone that I knew that I had died and begun a trip to heaven, they all thought I was nuts. [She told a long, involved story about her first "trip to heaven," and I analyzed it as a typical NDE.]

> Well, I had these devastating attacks several times, and once, when I was recovering in a special room, I felt better and when no one came to see how I was, I just got up and got to

wandering down the hall. I went into a room where I thought I heard voices, and it was dark. I put out my hands in front of me and I felt lots of instruments. I just picked up one to hold out in front of me while I looked for the light switch, and all of a sudden there was a man screaming. I heard a woman, too, but the doctor said he was alone. . . .

I was pretty well drugged out after that, and the next thing I remember was living in a hospital with bars on the windows and my door was locked. No one wanted to tell me what happened, but finally a nurse did, and I was shocked. I never tried to kill my doctor! But they had my medical records, and I was down as a nut. So off I went. I guess that's better than going to prison, but it was all so unfair. My cousin's next door neighbor is a lawyer, and I told him about what happened, and he said it would be an awful expensive case, and he couldn't take the time to investigate for nothing. . . .

My life is just short-circuited now. I had an apartment which was rented out to someone else when I was put away, and I don't get any answer from the address where I sent my rent check. The only person I see is a psychiatrist now, and when I tried to tell him that this all started when I was dead and was going to heaven, well, he just lit up a cigarette and smiled. That doesn't help me much, especially when I need a place to live and food to eat, and my things back from my apartment. My bank book is gone, and so are all my personal papers. The bank said someone would investigate, but I sat there all one day and no one did. Do you think it was unreasonable for me to think that the hospital social worker would help me? She said it wasn't her job. Well, whose job is it? I don't have anyone. I feel like I've been a victim of just about everyone, and when I said *that* to the psychiatrist, he asked if I meant my parents, too. I told him he was a jerk. That didn't go over too well, either. . . .

I've just been hanging around this mall so I had a place to sit and find food. I eat in the market, and I feel guilty about that, but I see teenagers eating ice creams and muffins and drinking sodas, and they're wearing expensive clothes, so I try not to think about what I have to do. . . .

I called a hotline today, and they said I can stay in a motel for one night, but what good is that going to do me? I need someone to pay attention to me. I'm not nuts, I never was, but I sure as hell am going to be after another week of this
. . . .

Bea articulates the variety of problems which can accumulate after an initial episode of misdiagnosis and/or misunderstanding. Disregarding the rather pointed allusion to misbehavior and a cover-up by the doctor, it can be seen that a near-death experience which was ignored initiated a landslide of circumstances which led to homelessness.

Nell's (age 55, Baltimore County, Maryland, 1979) experiences focus on "labelling," or "earmarking" as a major problem:

I know that it sounds strange to say that I have been with aliens, but I'm not crazy and I'm perfectly willing to take a lie-detector test. I have been in communication with these extraterrestrials for about two years now, and I have been taken on a spaceship three times. Now I know that it is difficult to believe; don't you think I really thought about it long and hard before I told anyone?

It doesn't make it any easier to be homeless, because I'm naturally considered to be different before I say much. I can still remember being one of the respected members of my neighborhood, and it isn't my fault that my husband wanted to get rid of me for another woman and I ended up getting fucked-over by an attorney and not being allowed any support. So when I was living in back of the old Ma and Pa railroad station—and creeping into the little closed building at night to keep warm—I saw these lights and right there in the hills a spaceship landed. I watched these peculiar creatures taking some samples from the earth and measuring—the air, I guess—with some instruments for two nights. During the day the ship just sort of became invisible; the lights are the only thing that seem to create visibility. Then I suppose I got in the measurement, and I was pulled into a beam of blue-white light and drifted to the ship. It's since been sort of examinations—probings—and some manner of soundless communicating, but with strange clicking noises which I can't seem to place as being from the beings or the instruments.

But that's not what I want to tell you about. It's how I've been treated. Now I know that I sound mad, but I'm not. I'm really low, it's true, and I get too blue some days. I can't seem to get rid of it sometimes. . . .

I didn't *have* to tell anyone what happened.

There must be people who are interested in hearing about my experiences, and there must be studies being done. No one believes me, and I don't get the respect that someone who isn't homeless gets. All I want is to have someone who has some experience in these matters to listen to me without just shoving me away as a crazy lady. I asked if there was some expert I could talk to, and all I got was a psychiatrist who gave me a bottle of pills and said I should get welfare to pay for refills. I've been labelled, and it's all downhill from there. *Once labelled, always inabled,* I say. (italics added)

Conscious or unconscious memories reveal beliefs which can be traced in tradition and understood in the proper perspective. But often characters related to legendry become confused with related others. "Death personified" may interchange character with Satan; a revenant may be confused with a "Poor Soul" (the difference being that the revenant returns from death temporarily to accomplish some deed and the Poor Soul wanders the land forever); and "spirits" may be called Will-o'-the-Wisps or Jack-O-Lanterns. It is especially important, then, that listeners understand that any believed encounter with the supernatural may generate storytellings which do not make sense to the general public but have had a profound effect on the victim's life. Bonnie (age 47, Hollywood, California, 1985) is sure that the old home in which she lives (as a squatter) is haunted and that the hills behind the house are inhabited by spirits:

> I know there is a ghost in the house. I think that the person who died here is looking for something lost and has returned for it. If the ghost can be satisfied, then he can rest in peace. The reason I think that is because all of the action is in pulling out drawers and moving things. It's the kind of thing I'd do if I were looking for something. I remember that my grandmother, who was from England, used to sing two songs—one about some man who came back from the dead to do something he'd forgotten to do and the other about a woman who returned to earth to quiet a sobbing lover—and this reminds me of those. I've tried to remember how to help the ghost, but I didn't pay much attention to what my grandmother said. I had one awful time when I was sick with the mumps and she took care of me. She kept telling me about the demons who carried lanterns and made you follow them to death. [I believe she means Jack-O-Lanterns.] I never got to talk about them to her because she was afraid of them. I think she thought that they knew she was aware of them and that made her a target. I've been afraid of talking about that time, too. [I have deleted some interesting but lengthy tales about experiences with her grandmother.]
>
> Then there's the matter of the spirits that carry lights and try to lure me into the trees. I started to follow them one night and got scared and went and hid in a closet where there weren't any windows and the light couldn't get to me. It doesn't have anything to do with me—I hope! And the hill spirits are restless, wandering and trying to get someone to come to them, maybe, though, to die. All kinds of different and spooky places are where otherworld creatures live. The hills in back of the house are loaded with odd nooks and crannies and dark, cold, breezy places.

I told a doctor at the clinic about the ghost and the spirits, and he started writing real fast. From that day on, all he does is nod and smile at me. He gives me pills and won't even let me talk about what I see and hear. He acts like I'm an incurable patient. Well, I know what I see and hear, and if it isn't a ghost and spirits, then what is it? I get depressed just thinking about how I feel and that I have no one to tell. The pills make me more depressed.

Why can't we have set-up groups of women who get together and discuss what's bothering us? There must be plenty that's got problems that others share and maybe we get them from childhood and the people who were involved in our upbringing.

Then the doctors wouldn't have to listen to us, and we'd be able to help each other.

If mental health professionals do not establish support groups for the sharing of such experiences, then the church can provide the setting and opportunity for storytellings. When "we" understand that these unusual experiences are believed to be just as depicted, and we observe that the tellers are not dysfunctionally mentally ill, there is no reason to isolate these women or treat them any differently than the women who do not report supranormal experiences. The *first* step for many churchwomen, then, may be that opportunity for idle conversation after an informal meal in the church hall. Chatting leads to storytelling, and from those stories it can be determined if a support group will be attended. The group can be called something very simple, like "Women Sharing Experiences."

5. The Churchwomen's Movement

Joanne (age 63, Los Angeles, California, 1987) sat across the street from a large Catholic church and mused:

There's that big Catholic church over there. What a waste. Such big congregations every Sunday, and then if bingo doesn't get them in during the week, it's sleepy-time all over the country. . . .

You know, with this new computer age, it would be easy for them to just hook up with each other all over the state and country and make a united effort to feed, clothe, and house all us unfortunate women. We could move about, too.

Do you think the women who belong to the Catholic Charities ever thought of taking over like that? It's a cinch that no one is going to invite *me* in to make any suggestions! And I could bring in a dozen more like me to tell them how we figure on changing the wrongs that are goin' on. But no one values what we think. No one figures that we *do* think. But we know more because we *live* it. . . .

There were so many similar stories that I could not ignore them. In my doctoral dissertation I proposed a multi-level plan to establish a telecommunication system for relocating women to urban and rural areas of their choice—where there would be organizations prepared to receive and direct them. "Resituation" services at the neighborhood church level would include housemate "matchmaking" for the purpose of sharing homes and resources; taking a newcomer to the local branch of the state vocational rehabilitation office for evaluation regarding job (re)training; escorting a woman to a church and introducing her to "new friends"; inviting those who have compatible interests to weekly community events; providing information about local transportation; locating needed or desired health and educational programs; finding and/or forming appropriate groups to satisfy aesthetic, social, spiritual, and political needs; and teaching classes in home economics, art, meditation, physical fitness, gardening, and how to obtain government benefits—particularly in regard to the various programs of the Social Security Act.

The base of operations is the *neighborhood* church, where members daily see and hear what is happening in their own community; women know the social, political, and economic situations in their home, work, and play environments. They engage in face-to-face interaction with school, law, public safety, bank, and business staff. Without conscious effort, they are involved deeply in a community outreach program. They are especially effective because they *personalize* their messages. And the church is a solid organizational base from which to evoke cooperation from the most disinterested or stubborn member of "the opposition." Resourcing, then—the gathering and pooling of invaluable information and personnel—is a natural activity in one's own community. The neighborhood is also the origin of strategy for influence and power: information-passing in newsletters and newspapers, posters, letters to and appearances before the City Council, press conferences at the Press Club, publicity releases, guesting on a local television show, and filing complaints against corrupt officials. At this early stage, it is advantageous to learn about purchasing probate property (and other real estate strategies), socially responsible investing, and local networks for ecologically-sound home building techniques (as in solar panels, etc.). These tools are all applicable to assisting the homeless at the churchwoman's (neighborhood) level.

What cannot be accomplished by the members of one church is usually attainable by networking with other *community* churches. Key people come together to focus on particular needs, and resourcing grows and is used by committed participants as a tool to communicate similar or correlating problems and improvements. Coalitions are formed as representatives of diverse groups see the opportunity for cooperative ventures. This is the time to learn more about how to organize a community land trust if land use and a need for affordable housing (often associated with local employment problems) are issues.

Churchwomen who are experts on their own communities can be of immense value at the *regional* level of interfacing. Joining forces means being able to address larger projects, such as the exchange of various organizational information, personnel, and tangibles for the purpose of forming a small self-sufficiency group—a cooperative venture in housing, crops, and jobbing—if a community land trust is not applicable. Experts in all fields can move within one region to instruct, assist, and learn new methods and techniques to pass along elsewhere. Resourcing will have developed into a major project which is shared in oral communication, writing, and video while being stored and updated in computer "bulletin boards."

When regional representatives get together, they should be planning what they can add to *national* conferences. The concerns and programs of the local, community, and regional levels are combined when members meet for national networking. By this time it is a webwork of information and personnel sharing. Brainstorming sessions at national meetings culminate in greater power: national media attention, support (or the lack of it) for certain political candidates, larger fund-raisers, and lobbying ability. All of the areas in which women can help each other obtain self-reliance will be addressed, and the opportunity for creating a *national* network of self-sufficiency communities which constantly exchange knowledge and physical assistance moves from "talk" to the development stage. Each local churchwoman has been effective in some way; her multiple life-identities reach their highest potential as she shares her God-given gifts for the betterment of the situations in which other women are caught and which she may, quite unexpectedly, one day experience herself.

When other national coalitions have conferences on the state of human and environmental progress, there will be new representatives from a churchwomen's movement to point to achievements which have escaped the attention of others. By focusing on the effects of and solutions to victimization, poverty, and homelessness, people who were once without hope can come forward to testify to the power of working together in spiritual harmony through the auspices of local houses of worship. That special persona—"religious woman"—can bridge the separatist attitudes and actions that are destroying family life and the fabric of our society.

Appendix

Exhibit 1.

Hand delivered postponement request by Rubin Bard's attorney for the only postponement of the trial.

Law Offices

**Nolan, Plumhoff & Williams
Chartered**

204 West Pennsylvania Avenue

Towson, Maryland 21204

J. Earle Plumhoff
Newton A. Williams
William M. Hesson, Jr.
Thomas J. Renner
Kenneth H. Masters
Stephen J. Nolan
William P. Englehart, Jr.
Jean M. Sadowsky

Area Code 301
Telephone
823-7600

January 26, 1982

Hand Delivered

Ms. Irene Summers
Assignment Office
Circuit Court for Baltimore County
County Courts Building
Towson, Maryland 21204

Re: *Bard v. Bard*, Equity No. 111277

Dear Ms. Summers:

I received today a copy of the trial notice for the above-captioned contested divorce proceeding, scheduling the same for Tuesday, April 12, 1983 at 9:30 a.m. Due to a conflict, I am respectfully requesting that this case be rescheduled for a trial date on or after May 3, 1983.

I greatly appreciate your kind assistance in this matter.

Very truly yours,

Stephen J. Nolan

SJN: jka
oc: Marjorie Brook Bard
Mr. Rubin Bard

Exhibit 2.

Denial of Marjorie Bard's postponement request by Irene Summers on the grounds that the previous postponement was requested by her and provided for her.

Form CA2

CIRCUIT COURT FOR BALTIMORE COUNTY

Tobi Adams - 494-2660
Civil Assignment Commissioner
Settlement Court

Maria Ercolano - 494-2662
Masters Assignment Clerk
Medical Records

ASSIGNMENT OFFICE
COUNTY COURTS BUILDING
401 Bosley Avenue
P.O. Box 6754
Towson, Maryland, 21204-0754
March 16, 1983

Kathy Rushion - 494-2660
Assignment - Jury - Motions
Marcia Fennell
Assistant Clerk Typist
Irene Summers - 494-2661
Assignment - Non-Jury - Motions
Freddie Grove
Assistant Clerk Typist

To: Stephen J. Nolan, Esq.
        M's Marjorie Brook Bard (P')

Note: Confirming notice that the above cited case remains in the assignment for trial on its merits for Tuesday, May 3, 1983, @9:30 a.m. Defendant's request for postponement has been denied due to the previous postponement was for the same reason, without variation.

RE: EQUITY - 111277 - BARD VS. BARD

HEARING DATE: Tuesday, May 3, 1983, @9:30 a.m.

ON THE FOLLOWING: Merits: 1 hour